W9-BEO-204

THE INTEGRATED
PHYSICAL SECURITY HANDBOOK II

Second Edition

Written & Compiled by:
Don Philpott & Shuki Einstein

Government Training Inc.™

Published by
Government Training Inc.™
ISBN: 978-0-9832361-0-8

About the Publisher – Government Training Inc. ™

Government Training Inc. provides worldwide training, publishing and consulting to government agencies and contractors that support government in areas of business and financial management, acquisition and contracting, physical and cyber security and intelligence operations. Our management team and instructors are seasoned executives with demonstrated experience in areas of Federal, State, Local and DoD needs and mandates.

Recent books published by Government Training Inc. ™ include:

☐ Securing Our Schools

☐ Workplace Violence

☐ The Grant Writer's Handbook

☐ The Integrated Physical Security Handbook (First Edition)

☐ Handbook for Managing Teleworkers

☐ Handbook for Managing Teleworkers: Toolkit

☐ Small Business Guide to Government Contracting

For more information on the company, its publications and professional training, go to www.GovernmentTrainingInc.com.

Copyright © 2011 Government Training Inc. All rights reserved.

Printed in the United States of America.

This publication is protected by copyright, and permission must be obtained from the publisher prior to any prohibited reproduction, storage in a retrieval system or transmission in any form or by any means, electronic, mechanical, photocopying, recording or likewise.

For information regarding permissions, write to:

Government Training Inc. ™

Rights and Contracts Department

5372 Sandhamn Place

Longboat Key, Florida 34228

don.dickson@GovernmentTrainingInc.com

ISBN: 978-0-9832361-0-8

www.GovernmentTrainingInc.com

ACKNOWLEDGEMENTS

This manual has drawn heavily on the authoritative materials published by the Federal Emergency Management Agency (FEMA), the Department of Homeland Security (DHS), Government Accountability Office (GAO),General Services Administration (GSA), and Headquarters, Department of the Army. These materials are in the public domain but accreditation has been given both in the text and in the reference section if you need additional information. Finally, the publishers wish to acknowledge the considerable contribution from CH2M Hill security consultants security consultants, architects and engineers, with special thanks to Michael Chritton and Forrest Gist.

About the authors

Don Philpott

Don Philpott is editor of International Homeland Security Journal and has been writing, reporting and broadcasting on international events, trouble spots and major news stories for almost 40 years. For 20 years he was a senior correspondent with Press Association -Reuters, the wire service, and traveled the world on assignments including Northern Ireland, Lebanon, Israel, South Africa and Asia.

He writes for magazines and newspapers in the United States and Europe and is a regular contributor to radio and television programs on security and other issues. He is the author of more than 80 books on a wide range of subjects and has had more than 5,000 articles printed in publications around the world. His most recent books are "Terror - Is America Safe?", The Wounded Warrior Handbook, Workplace Violence Prevention and the Education Facility Security Handbook. He has written special reports on "Protecting the Athens Olympics", "The Threat from Dirty Bombs", "Anti-Terrorism Measures in the UK", "Nanotechnology and the U.S. Military" and "The Global Impact of the London Bombings."

Born in the UK he is now an American citizen working out of Orlando, Florida.

Shuki Einstein

Shuki Einstein, LEEDAP, International Associate AIA, is an architect and an internationally recognized security expert and strategic planner with more than 25 years' experience. Born in New York he moved to Jerusalem at the age of 9. He served in the Israel Defense Force, trained as an architect at the Technion – Israel Institute of Technology in Haifa and practiced as a licensed architect in Israel for 14 years. He was the CH2M Hill Architectural Discipline Coordinator in the Middle East office before relocating with his family to Portland, Ore., in 2000. Currently he is Global Architectural Discipline Manager and Best Practice Leader.

His design experience has included numerous complex projects involving integrated multidisciplinary design, from front-end conceptual design to development of construction documentation. In addition to traditional architectural design, his experience also includes master planning, interior design, and project management, and he has managed projects in Europe, the Middle East, Asia and North America.

He has extensive experience in integrating architectural physical protection systems with functionality, maintenance, operations and access control systems. He is a nationally recognized counterterrorism expert, consultant, and speaker, and his areas of expertise include vulnerability assessments, security master planning and security awareness training.

Einstein currently lives in Oregon, with his wife and three children.

Symbols

Throughout this book you will see a number of icons displayed in the margins. The icons are there to help you as you work through the Five Step process. Each icon acts as an advisory – for instance alerting you to things that you must always do or should never do. The icons used are:

Must Do   This is something that you must always do

No No   This is something you should never do

Tips   Really useful tips

Remember   Points to bear in mind

Checklist   Have you checked off or answered everything on this list?

CONTENTS

WORKSHEET SAMPLES*

*Blank worksheets can be found at the end of the book.

FOREWORD

Our nation and the world have changed dramatically since the tragic events of September 11. It is not just our facilities and institutions that are threatened; our freedoms and the quality of life that we hold so dear are also under attack.

We have the dual responsibility of ensuring that the facilities and buildings where we work and play are as secure as possible and at the same time, we have to maintain an acceptable quality of life.

Integrated physical security planning does not mean reverting to a bunker philosophy. It does, however, involve a sometimes difficult balancing act between effective and adequate security and being able to carry on business as usual.

Measures that have been and continue to be taken to protect and defend our homeland have made us all safer but we still live in troubled times.

Today's terrorists can strike at any place and at any time and with a wide variety of weapons.

Our critical infrastructures, like ports, power stations and water treatment plants, are an obvious target but so are millions of other facilities nationwide where tens of millions of Americans work every day.

There are also countless threats that we face, both natural and man-made – from hurricanes, floods and earthquakes to theft, workplace violence and serious crime - that need to be addressed.

Vulnerable facilities include local, state and federal government buildings and private offices, as well as schools, hospitals, places of worship, food outlets, malls, theaters and sports arenas.

While most of us take steps to protect our homes and our personal possessions, many facilities both public and private, do not receive the same security protection putting the buildings and assets – including the people who work and visit there - at risk.

Many facility managers have taken the view "It won't happen to me" - but it might. Even if your building is not a target, have you considered the consequences of an explosion at a nearby facility and how that would impact on your business and people?

That is why integrated physical security planning is so critical. Once you have identified the threats and vulnerabilities, you can prioritize the assets that need to be protected. You are then in a position to develop a physical security plan to defend them.

A secure facility is a safer facility and by working with local government, neighboring properties, law enforcement and fire, you can help in building safer and more secure communities.

The challenge is enormous but steadily we will prevail. The more facilities and buildings that implement integrated physical security systems, the safer we all become. This helps protect us against terrorism and disasters and make us safer and more secure. It is how we can all help build a better and stronger America – one facility at a time.

John A. Gordon, General

U.S. Air Force (Retired)

Formerly President's Homeland Security Advisor

INTRODUCTION

Protecting America One Facility at a Time

Overview

More than half the facilities in the United States do not have a crisis management plan – what to do in the event of an emergency - and many that do, do not keep it up to date. Even fewer businesses and organizations have integrated physical security plans to protect the facility and people who work in it.

While alarming, this statistic is not surprising. Until 9/11 most businesses and facilities took the attitude: "it will never happen to me". On 9/12, tens of thousands of managers across the country were called in by their bosses and told they were now responsible for facility security – some knew what was expected of them, others did not. Ten years on, that is still a major problem and that is what this handbook sets out to address.

The catastrophic effects of Hurricane Katrina and the subsequent flooding, the earthquake in Haiti and the devastating oil spill in the Gulf of Mexico are all somber reminders of just how critical good planning and preparedness is. The biggest mistake made by emergency managers planning for a Hurricane Katrina-type event in the Gulf States was that they made assumptions. They assumed the coastline would not get hit by anything above a Category 3 hurricane and they assumed the levees protecting New Orleans would hold. Both assumptions proved to be deadly errors. Never assume anything and especially never assume that it can't happen to you. The process of developing an Integrated Physical Security plan demands that you consider all conceivable threats, even the doomsday ones, so that you can come up with effective plans to mitigate them. That is the only way to protect our nation's facilities and the people who work in them.

The Challenge

Remember

The challenge is two fold. The first challenge is to get agreement that something needs to be done. This involves altering mindsets; building consensus and getting senior management buy in. The second challenge is in developing and implementing an effective and tailor-made integrated physical security (IPS) plan. This plan consists of three mutually supporting elements –

☐ Physical security measures

☐ Operational procedures

☐ Policies.

Physical security covers all the devices, technologies and specialist materials for perimeter, external and internal protection. This covers everything from sensors and closed circuit television to barriers, lighting and access controls.

Remember

Operational procedures are the lifeblood of any organization - they cover how the facility works on a day to day business, shift changes, deliveries, when maintenance is carried out and so on. You must understand how the facility works and operates in order to develop an effective integrated physical security plan that allows it to get on with its job with the least disruption as possible.

Equally you must recognize that any effective IPS is going to impact on operations – things will change and you have to both manage and plan for change and ensure that the reasons for the changes are understood and accepted by all personnel.

Policies spell out who does what and the actions to be taken to prevent an attack or incident, or should one take place to mitigate its impact and ensure continuation of business.

This handbook is designed to walk you through a five steps process. It will tell you what needs to be done and why and then tell you how to do it.

★ THE FIVE STEP PROCESS ★

1. **Step 1:** Your Model Secure Facility

2. **Step 2:** Gap Analysis

3. **Step 3:** Gap Closure

4. **Step 4:** Strategic Plan

5. **Step 5:** Implementation

Ultimately almost any IPS is a compromise because you can't make a facility 100% secure if you have a continual flow of people and vehicles coming in and out. The aim, however, must be to develop an integrated physical security program that meets all key objectives and provides the maximum protection against defined threats with the resources available.

Must Do

The other major consideration is in knowing when enough is enough. It is possible to keep adding enhancements and new security levels but again, there has to be a compromise. At what point does there cease to be a quantifiable benefit in spending more money, especially if the security levels become so stringent that they impact your ability to conduct business as usual.

The goal of implementing an integrated physical security plan is in achieving sensible security, sustainable security.

Tips

A secure facility is a safer facility and by achieving this you boost morale and wellbeing.

The goal of this handbook is in making all our facilities and buildings secure and safe while maintaining in our offices and workplaces the quality of life that we have come to expect over many years. Our target is making America safer – one facility at a time.

This Five Step Process enables you to understand the different elements that need to be considered when developing your integrated physical security plan. Essential to these elements are who and what we are protecting:

- ☐ **People** – the people that work in and visit the facility, those working and living nearby and those who rely on your products and services.
- ☐ **Operations** – the day to day running of the facility covering everything from shifts and deliveries to maintenance and utilities.
- ☐ **Information** – information/data sources and protection, communications internally and externally.
- ☐ **Assets** – other than people cover anything that is key to your mission that can be destroyed, damaged or stolen, and
- ☐ **Inter-dependence** – how what happens at your facility may impact on the wider community and how incidents at neighboring facilities might impact on you. You have to be aware of what is happening upstream and downstream of your facility.

When developing a plan each of these categories has to be protected and the relationship between each has to be taken into account. As a result, a model security facility is one where all necessary systems are in place, tried and tested, to protect people, operations, inter-dependence and information without impacting on day to day operations. It is one where everyone knows why the systems are in place and what they have to do. It is a facility where confidence levels are high and people feel safe and secure.

Remember

Striking the Right Balance

As you go through this manual you will notice a lot of different levels of detail. It is your choice how deep you want to go and that will depend on a number of factors. These include how much you already know, the threat level to your facility, the complexity of the facility i.e. does it have multiple tiers of security, and your access to advice from in-house or external experts.

Tips

The key challenge in implementing IPS is to do the maximum necessary to ensure the safety and security of the facility and the critical assets within, without impacting on the day to day operational procedures. There is no benefit in implementing draconian security measures if they are so restrictive that the facility cannot function normally or if the people they are supposed to protect feel threatened by them. Equally there is little point in introducing hugely expensive security measures if a) the cost's can't be justified, b) the measures are not justified, or both.

A good example of NOT striking the right balance is the facility manager who goes out and buys a number of security cameras, which he has installed around the building. While the presence of highly visible cameras might increase safety levels, they are not completely effective unless someone is monitoring them – and this had not been taken into account. Who was going to monitor the cameras, how were these people going to be trained, where was the monitoring station to be located, how many monitors would it have, what protocols were in place to initiate a security response etc. etc? Having hired and trained monitoring staff, did the overall cost justify installation of the cameras in the first place or would a security guard walking around the facility every couple of hours have been as effective?

Integrated physical security plans are by their very nature a compromise – a careful balancing act between what needs to be done and what can be done weighed against what is in the best interest of the facility and its normal day to day procedures.

Communications

Must Do

Integrated physical security planning should not be undertaken in isolation. While you are developing the most effective plan for your facility, investigate what similar facilities have done or are doing, speak with security experts and first responders to get their input. Discuss your plans with your insurance company – after all, they have a vested interest in reducing their liability so they may be willing to reduce your premiums if you implement security measures and in some cases, they might even be willing to contribute towards the cost.

It is this communication between facilities and external stakeholders that will enable everyone to share information and help develop best practices nationwide. And, with these communication paths open you will be better able to protect your facility and thus help protect our nation – one building at a time. However, this does raise a paradox – you have to have open communications to ensure stakeholders know what is happening, yet you also have to ensure security so that details about what you are doing does not fall into the wrong hands.

Introduction

Terrorism is not a new challenge and it is not going to go away any time soon as the events in recent years in Times Square, New York, London, Madrid and Mumbai so graphically illustrated. So we have a duty to ensure that the places where we work, learn and play are secure and that the people using them are safe.

Integrated physical security planning is also important because risks come from both natural disasters such as earthquakes, floods and hurricanes as well as man-made threats ranging from theft to terrorism.

Vulnerable facilities are buildings that have a gap between their mission and their identified risks.

Remember

These include many critical infrastructures such as power plants, water treatment works and food processing plants. They also include local, state and federal government buildings and private offices where we work, the schools where our children are taught, the hospitals where we are treated, the churches where we worship, the restaurants where we eat and the malls where we shop.

Many of the facilities most at risk are in urban settings because they do not have enough property to establish robust perimeters – i.e. set back far enough from the road to prevent or mitigate the effects of a car bomb. It is the integrated physical protection of these facilities that this handbook focuses on.

Why You Need It

Integrated physical security is a must. Apart from the legal and liability issues, it just makes sense to protect the facilities and people on whom you depend - to keep your enterprise safe and secure so that you can, hopefully, prevent an attack but if one does happen, survive it.

Must Do

For many organizations there are also added benefits from implementing IPS. During the risk and threat assessment phases of developing an IPS, you frequently discover areas of vulnerability that can be remedied and practices that can be improved. This can lead to improved productivity and efficiency and this has an ongoing impact on your bottom line. So by implementing an IPS, you may also increase efficiency and profitability.

The biggest benefit, however, is in increased safety for everyone using that facility. It is essential to effectively communicate the need for the IPS to all concerned and to get them actively involved in the process. After all, one of the cheapest forms of physical security – and among the most effective – are the eyes and ears of the people using the facility.

Remember

If people understand the need for vigilance and report anything suspicious, they will all feel safer and more secure.

And people need to feel safe and secure.

We will "hit hard the American economy at its heart and its core." - Osama bin Laden

The terrorist threat does not only come from overseas. According to the FBI, there are more than 1,000 pipe bomb incidents every year. In the last ten years more than 80 students, teachers and custodians have been shot dead at incidents in schools. The threat is real and growing.

The Five Step Process

This Five Step Process is based on the IPS methodology developed by Denver-based CH2M Hill, one of the world's leading integrated design companies. The handbook walks you through the five steps needed to identify critical assets, identify threats and targets and take the appropriate mitigating measures in order to implement an effective integrated physical security system that addresses your specific needs and requirements.

It must be stressed that this handbook addresses integrated physical security. Physical security is the protection of buildings and all its assets, including people.

Remember Integrated physical security recognizes that optimum protection comes from three mutually supporting elements – physical security measures, operational procedures and procedural security measures and that is what this five step methodology is based on.

In some cases costly physical security measures can be avoided by simple changes to operational procedures. In other instances, the implementation of physical security measures can greatly increase operating efficiency with significant bottom line benefits.

THE FIVE STEP PROCESS

★ THE FIVE STEP PROCESS ★

1. **Step 1:** Your Model Secure Facility

2. **Step 2:** Gap Analysis

3. **Step 3:** Gap Closure

4. **Step 4:** Strategic Plan

5. **Step 5:** Implementation

Introduction

In order to carry out a comprehensive assessment of what your facility needs, you have to understand the basic elements of security - what it is you are protecting and how vulnerable it is. You have to know where any threats may come from and what you can do to prevent them or mitigate them. You have to understand the principles of deterrence, detection, delay, response, recovery and re-evaluation. You need to be aware of all the options available to you. Armed with this knowledge you can develop and implement the most appropriate integrated physical security plan for your facility.

Must Do

When planning, there are really two scenarios – if and when. The "if" scenario covers planning and procedures to prevent the likelihood of an incident. The "when" scenario covers planning and procedures after an incident and is mainly concerned with mitigation and recovery.

Remember that the cost to mitigate and recover may be less than the cost to protect so there always has to be a balance between protection and mitigation.

In effect, IPS is a series of countermeasures to prevent or reduce the impact of an attack. And, as mentioned before, IPS has to be balanced against cost and any disadvantages. Extreme security countermeasures should not be implemented if they disrupt operations or adversely affect the safety of the occupants of a building. For instance, a poorly designed access controlled door might slow down the evacuation of a building in the event of an emergency.

Remember

That is why when designing IPS, you determine objectives and create a plan and then you assess and analyze the design again before implementing it. The plan should contain the following crucial elements – DDDRRR - deterrence, detection, delay, response, recovery and re-evaluation. These are discussed in greater detail in Security 101 if you need to refer to this and they are an integral part of your PSS.

☐ Deterrence provides countermeasures such as policies, procedures, and technical devices and controls to defend against attacks on the assets being protected.

☐ Detection monitors for potential breakdowns in protective mechanisms that could result in security breaches or compromising security zones/layers.

☐ Delay -If there is a breach, measures are needed to delay the intruders long enough to allow a security team to apprehend them before they achieve their objective.

☐ Response, which requires human involvement, covers procedures and actions for assessing the situation and responding to a breach. Note: Because absolute protection is impossible to achieve, a security program that does not also incorporate detection, delay and response is incomplete. To be effective, all three concepts must be elements of a cycle that work together continuously.

☐ Recovery is your plan to continue business and operations as normally as possible following an incident, and

☐ Re-evaluation is critical. You must constantly keep your PSS under review and keep revisiting your original assessment and objectives. Has the situation changed, do you now face new threats, what must be done to ensure the PSS continues to meet your goals and objectives.

Each of these elements has to be planned in relationship to all the others. There is no point in spending money on expensive perimeter fences if there is no detection system in place to warn of intrusion. There is no point in installing sophisticated detection systems if there is nobody around to respond to them if they trigger an alarm. And, there is little point in having deterrence and detection without delay if an intruder can gain access, cause damage and get away because there were no delaying measures in place or response times were too slow.

You must understand what you are protecting and from whom. You should never go out and spend money on hardware until you are certain that you are going to achieve the objectives that you have set out.

Step One – Your Model Secure Facility

Now that you have an understanding of basic security techniques and applications relating to facility protection, we next look at a model secure facility – the facility that in a perfect world, is able to able to maximize security without compromising business as usual. Many methodologies omit this and go straight on to the different assessment processes that you need to undertake as you develop a strategic plan to implement an integrated physical security system. However, we believe it is important that you examine what would constitute a model secure facility for you. This is one which has identified its core functions, identified its critical assets, identified the threats and vulnerabilities and taken the appropriate measures to mitigate them. Above all, it is a facility that is secure yet one that is able to carry on its core function as efficiently and effectively as before the IPS was implemented. When you come up with your model facility, you have a benchmark for comparison.

Step Two - Gap Analysis – How do you compare with the model facility?

The goal of physical security is to protect facilities and buildings and the assets contained inside. The most important of these assets are, of course, the people who work in and visit the facility. The first things you need to find out are:

Remember

☐ The assets to be protected.

☐ The threat to those assets.

☐ The vulnerability of those assets

☐ My priorities

Fact: 85% of all critical infrastructures and key resources in the U.S. are privately-owned.

What Am I Protecting?

Protective systems should always be developed for specific assets. You have to know the core functions of your facility because that will enable you to identify the specific critical infrastructure that you need to protect in order to continue in business in the event of an attack.

Remember

The goal of security is to protect facilities and buildings and the assets contained inside. Various layers of security may be necessary in different parts of the building depending on the assets located there. For instance, there should be relatively free access to the office kitchen/lunch room but restricted access to the computer network control room.

Asset value is determined by considering the following three elements:

☐ The criticality of the asset for its user and/or others

☐ How easily the asset can be replaced.

☐ Some measure of the asset's relative value.

Assets are anything key to your mission that can be destroyed, damaged or stolen. The risk-analysis procedure is used to identify assets – everything from the building itself to hazardous materials, equipment, supplies, furniture, computers, IT infrastructure and, of course, people.

Who Are My Adversaries?

Tips

It is important to identify and characterize the threat to these assets. This threat can come from within or without the building. Internal threats include pilfering of office equipment or theft of classified information. Internal threats also include disgruntled employees who may sabotage equipment or attack other employees. External threats range from vandalism and break-in thefts to acts of terrorism. You need to know your adversaries and the various tactics they might use. You also need to know their motivations and capabilities. Consult with your local police, the FBI and other agencies who monitor these threats. They can advise on what threats you face, from whom and what methods and weapons they might use. Two other tools you can use are:

Design Base Threat (DBT) analysis to help identify your likely adversaries, their strengths and capabilities, what their targets might be and the likelihood of them attacking you and if so, how.

Crime Prevention Through Environmental Design (CPTED) – is one of the tried and trusted methodologies available to you. It takes into account the relationship between the physical environment and the users of that environment. It is a useful tool in identifying the bad boys and what crimes may impact on your facility and personnel.

Where am I vulnerable?

Must Do

Until you discover your areas of vulnerability, you cannot develop the strategies needed to protect them. A useful way of identifying threats to conduct scenario based assessments. This is a very analytical process because you must be able to identify all critical flaws and weak points in your current physical protection. You have to come up with multiple "what if" scenarios and work them through. By working through the various scenarios and determining the probable actions and consequences, you can then develop plans to counter or mitigate them.

Use the model facility as your benchmark to identify the areas that need attention. Conduct an audit of the facility – site boundaries, building construction, room locations, access points, operating conditions (working hours, off-hours and so on), existing physical protection features, safety considerations and types and numbers of employees and visitors.

Next, determine all critical assets – tangible and intangible, equipment, personnel and materials. This analysis should also include reputation, morale and proprietary information.

Remember

You must identify and characterize vulnerabilities – weaknesses - that would allow identified threats to be realized. A major problem for buildings in urban areas is lack of a secure perimeter. In many situations a vehicle containing a bomb could park within feet of a building causing major damage on detonation. Internal vulnerabilities include poorly trained security staff and lack of access controls to sensitive parts of the building.

Also, assess how you might be impacted by an incident at a nearby facility – a chemical spill for instance - and what steps you would need to take to protect your property and people.

By identifying your weaknesses you are able to develop solutions to eliminate them.

What Are My Priorities?

Risk assessment must take into account the impact on your business or operation if assets are destroyed or damaged. Part of that assessment is to rate the impact of the loss of those assets on a scale of low, medium or high. This will identify the critical assets that need maximum protection.

How do I compare?

Once you have established the above, you are in a position to do your Gap Analysis to identify what needs to be done to reduce risk, increase safety and provide the necessary physical security for your building and people. How do you compare to the model facility, what are your threats and vulnerabilities? And, having identified these threats and vulnerabilities, how do you prioritize them – which are the most critical and must be tackled first.

Step Three - Gap Closure

Having identified your shortfalls, you must then consider and evaluate all available options to mitigate the threats. There is a vast array of external and internal systems and devices available. You must determine which are the best options and combinations for your particular circumstances. If you have questions, consult an independent security consultant rather than a vender with a vested interested in selling you its product.

Must Do

The options are described in general terms in Step Three and in more detail in Security 101.

☐ **Perimeter Security**

- How to secure the perimeter, perimeter surveillance, protection basics, defense measures, stand off distances and countermeasures to reduce security risks.

☐ **Vehicles**

- Protecting approaches, control access and parking, install barriers, surveillance and other monitoring equipment.

☐ **Internal Security**

- Access controls, alarms and barriers, authentication devices and screening, access biometrics, CCTV, hot site protection, safe mail rooms, coping with hazards and so on.

☐ **IT**

- Integrating IT, cyber and physical security planning, providing network/infrastructure protection and protecting files, document and other critical resources.

☐ **People**

- Security Staff - needs/hiring/training, security programs and responses
- Staff/visitors - screening/training/informing; drills/evacuation/safe rooms; alarms/ staging areas; communications and coping with and recovering from an event.
- Special needs - ADA requirements and special resources.

☐ **Building Design/Security**

- Building Code laws, exits/fences/gates/doors/barriers; windows, critical floor space/safe rooms/safe areas; devices/detectors; lighting, cameras and maintenance.

☐ **Community Risk Assessment/Community Involvement**

- Assessing local risks and incorporating into planning; working with fire/police/EM, working with the local business community and working with local community.

☐ **Technology Solutions**

The handbook deals with the various security and defense devices available to you. These are referred to in Security 101 and the Gap Analysis and Gap Closure chapters but not in as much technical detail as you may wish. References are provided throughout the book to allow you to get more comprehensive information should you need it.

Step Four - Strategic Plan

Having identified assets, adversaries, threats, vulnerabilities and determined priorities and options, you are in a position to plan and strategize the security change process. This means developing a road map – you know where you are and you have to plot how you are going to get where you need to be.

The strategic plan sets out Steps Two and Three above – documenting your Gap Analysis, identifying critical assets, threats and weaknesses and all areas needing to be addressed. The Gap Closure documents how you plan to close those gaps, the justification for the actions to be taken, costs involved and timeframe for implementation.

Remember

The strategic plan serves two critical functions – it is the marketing tool you need to get management approval and it is the blueprint for your physical security plan.

Step Five - Implementation

Once your Strategic Plan has been approved, it must be implemented. This includes project management, bid contracting and vendor selection, quality assurance and quality control and revising policy procedures.

Remember

Integrated Physical Security planning is also an ongoing requirement. Once your system is in place you must continuously test it for weaknesses and vulnerabilities. You must ensure your employees understand why the measures are in place and what they must do in the event of an emergency.

Re-analyze – what is my current situation? Ask yourself what has changed and what new threats have emerged. By constantly tracking and monitoring your integrated physical security system you can close any gaps and introduce enhancements.

Taken together, these five steps will allow you to understand the methodology needed to design and implement effective IPS and then maintain it to ensure that your building, its assets and its people remain safe and secure.

Summary

The Integrated Physical Security Handbook is the essential handbook for facility security managers and all managers and supervisors tasked with the security and safety of the buildings in which they operate and the people with whom they work. It sets out how to manage change and how to conduct crucial threat and risk assessments, the basis for all integrated physical security planning.

Then, using checklists, and standard practices it provides a hands-on, how to guide that leads you in a user-friendly way through all the steps and processes needed to evaluate, design and implement an effective integrated physical security system.

The handbook is a preparedness tool that could help protect lives and ensure the continuation of our businesses, institutions and critical infrastructures in the event of a terrorist attack or other major emergency. As a result it is a handbook that you cannot afford to be without.

The Current Situation – How Secure Are You?

There are:

More than 635,000 government-owned buildings and thousands more leased locations throughout the 50 states and Washington D.C., employing almost a million federal workers and hosting tens of millions of visitors.

They employ almost a million Federal workers and host tens of millions of visitors.

327,000 education buildings in the 50 states and D.C. There are 95,726 schools with 47 million children enrolled and employing approximately 3 million teachers.

7,569 hospitals nationwide employing 2.4 million registered nurses, 1.8 million nursing aides, 819,000 physicians and surgeons, 350,000 therapists. On any given day there are 539,000 hospital inpatients plus visitors.

127,000 additional health care facilities nationwide offering inpatient/outpatient treatment.

133,000 malls and strip malls and 534,000 large stores nationwide.

More than 1 million office buildings nationwide.

305,000 public assembly buildings nationwide.

307,000 churches nationwide.

603,000 warehouses and storage facilities nationwide.

349,000 food service facilities nationwide.

153,000 hotels and motels nationwide.

How many of these buildings and facilities have an effective physical security system in place?

How secure is your facility?

Step One: The Model Facility

Overview

Remember

> The model secure facility is one where all critical assets have been identified, the threats to them identified and prioritized and effective security measures put in place to mitigate them. All this has been done in consultation with all outside stakeholders including first responders, and in compliance with local, state and federal mandated requirements and all appropriate regulatory drivers. Above all, the physical security plan has been implemented with management and employee buy-in, to budget and on time with minimum ongoing disruption to the facility's day to day operating procedures.

Of course, this is the ideal situation but let us assume that you have been tasked with designing and implementing the perfect physical security plan. These are the steps you need to take.

Planning

Your aim in developing a model facility is to give you a benchmark to work with. By working your way through the Assessment Checklist and implementing the very best solution to each line item (where appropriate) you should finish up with the model integrated protection system for your facility. You can then compare your current situation with your model facility – the Gap Analysis - and see what needs be done to correct the situation.

Your purpose at this stage, however, is to develop the model facility and not to focus on the gaps which are dealt with in Step Two of our methodology.

> First you must set up your core team. This should include you as the project manager, the security and IT managers and all those who have responsibility for operational, building, system and maintenance functions in the facility.

Must Do

Together, the project team coordinates the preparation of the assessment schedule, assessment agenda, and on-site visit assessments with the building stakeholders. It is important to emphasize that the Team includes professionals capable of evaluating different parts of the buildings and familiar with engineering, architecture and site planning. Other members of the team should include security consultant, law-enforcement agents, first responders, building owners and managers and a representative from the facility's insurers.

Remember

From day one, the team must involve senior management so that they are aware of what is going on and the changes that will be coming so they can plan accordingly.

Throughout this process you must ensure:

☐ Confidentiality – the need to protect critical planning documents

☐ Appropriate PR – keeping the right people in the know while ensuring that information did not get into the wrong hands

☐ Sustainability – incorporating existing systems into the plan rather than replacing, implementing baseline security where appropriate, balancing physical protection systems with operational procedures

☐ Compliance with all industrial guidelines and legal, code and regulatory requirements

☐ Constant review and revision to accommodate new circumstances or threats

The Model Facility

Must Do

Remember that the aim in developing your model facility is to identify all critical assets – tangible and intangible – and reduce the risks to them to an acceptable level. You must take into account the following crucial elements – deterrence, detection, delay and response and then recovery and re-assessment – all are mitigation measures. These are the foundations on which any integrated physical security plan must be built. They create the vision for your secured facility.

☐ **Deterrence** - provides countermeasures such as policies, procedures, and technical devices and controls to defend against attacks on the assets being protected.

☐ **Detection** - monitors for potential breakdowns in protective mechanisms that could result in security breaches.

☐ **Delay** – provides measures that in the event of a breach, delays intruders long enough to allow a security team to apprehend them before they achieve their objective.

☐ **Response** - procedures and actions for responding to a breach. Note: Because total protection is almost impossible to achieve, a security program that does not also incorporate detection, delay and response is incomplete. To be effective, all three concepts must be elements of a cycle that work together continuously.

☐ **Recovery** - your plan to continue business and operations as normally as possible following an incident. Mitigation planning is part of your response and recovery with the aim of minimizing the effects of any incident.

☐ **Re-assessment** - crucial and an ongoing process. Before implementing any changes, you need to revisit your strategic plan to ensure that goals and objectives will be met. Whenever there are changed circumstances or when new threats are identified, revisit your strategic plan and conduct a re-assessment to see what additional measures, if any, are needed.

So now you can develop your own model secure facility. Work through the Assessment Checklist (see Step Five) and answer each question by coming up with the most ideal solution. Not all the questions may be relevant to your facility but for those that are, refer to the answers below to assist you in coming up with your best solutions.

1. What is your current security situation?

You must find out about the crime rate in your area, any current terrorist threats or alerts. You must know if your facility has been burgled or if threats have been made by present or former employees.

Must Do

We met with the local sheriff's department and discovered that there had been a number of assaults in the area late at night. We have notified this to all staff on shift duty and a security officer is available to escort members of staff to their vehicles if requested. We now liaise with the local police on a regular basis.

We have had several meetings with the local FBI office and members of the county homeland security team to keep abreast of terrorist threat alerts. A number of buildings in our neighborhood have been designated medium or high risk because of the nature of their work or materials stored on premises. We have taken the possible consequences of an attack on one of these buildings into account in developing our IPS.

We have conducted a thorough inventory of all materials stored onsite. Hazardous materials have been moved to a more secure area and locks and alarms have been installed on storerooms containing computers and other IT equipment.

Our facility was broken into about 18 months ago. Access was gained through a first floor window at the rear of the premises. All windows are now alarmed and there is nighttime external lighting around the building.

Signage at the front of the building was defaced by vandals. It has been replaced by graffiti-proof signs.

There has been only one case of workplace violence after an employee was disciplined for drinking on duty. Procedures have been revised so that counseling is available for employees both to prevent similar incidents and in response to them. Discussions take place on a regular basis between management and staff representatives on ways to reduce stress and tensions in the workplace.

Several attempts have been made to hack into our computer servers. We now employ an outside consultant who has instituted a number of IT security measures to protect the integrity of our systems. These security measures were introduced in tandem with our physical security upgrades as we were also installing close circuit television cameras with digital back up.

Until four years ago we had a sort of emergency plan in place but it wasn't reviewed on a regular basis. Now we have a comprehensive integrated physical security plan which is reviewed by the security team on a regular basis and is revised as needed. The plan was developed taking into account the company's emergency management plan and our COOP plan – how to stay in business after an attack.

2. Site - Neighbors

Must Do

You must review all the facilities in your neighborhood to see which, if any, pose a threat to you. Are there high-risk targets which might be attacked and if so, what would the impact be on your facility and your ability to continue operating.

We have identified all facilities in our area that pose a threat either as a target – there is an FBI office three blocks away - or because of the nature of their business – we have a distribution depot in the next street which houses toxic chemicals which could either be the target of a terrorist attack or pose a serious problem to us if there was a fire or spillage.

We have taken appropriate mitigating steps by physically strengthening our building where necessary and having on-site storage of solutions to counter any chemical spill. We have also consulted with the local fire department and the HAZMAT team who advised us on the correct procedures to follow in the event of an emergency.

We have a number of roads which run close to our facility. People in parked vehicles could use electronic devices to eavesdrop on what is going on or use weapons to fire at us or launch a grenade attack. We have erected fences to screen the facility from these vantage points.

3. Site – Location

Must Do

Walk around your perimeter and determine if your immediate surrounds are secure.

We determined that trees on our property could provide an attacker a vantage point either to spy on the facility or from which to launch an assault with a weapon. The trees have been removed giving us and the surveillance cameras a clear field of vision to and around our perimeter.

There is a lot of traffic – both vehicle and pedestrian - around our facility. Barriers were installed along our perimeter to prevent vehicles on nearby roads from crashing through our perimeter. Signs were erected warning pedestrians not to trespass on the property.

In one area vehicles were able to park on the road right alongside an external wall. After consultation with the police, this stretch of highway is now a no parking zone although it is still monitored by close circuit cameras.

4. Site – Perimeter

Focus on your perimeter – does it offer adequate protection, what are the vulnerabilities ?

The wire fence around the perimeter was damaged in several places and there were too many access points.

In some areas there is adequate stand off distance between the perimeter fence and the facilities main structure and in other areas the distance is not considered sufficient to provide protection from a bomb blast. In these areas there has been some physical hardening of the main building.

The fence has been replaced and strengthened in a number of places.

Lighting around the facility has been replaced to increase nighttime visibility.

The number of access points has been restricted to three, one for pedestrians and two for vehicles. All delivery vehicles now use one access point.

There are now guard posts at all three access points.

Signage has been improved around the perimeter including "Keep Out" signs.

Two manholes in the street just outside the facility have, in consultation with the utility company and the local authority, been secured by padlocks.

A subway line runs underneath the facility. Discussions with the local transit authority, have determined, however, that it is sufficiently deep underground not to pose a problem even in the event of a major explosion.

Our facility has underground parking and all access to it is controlled. The area is also monitored by CCTV and patrolled by security staff. Intercoms have also been installed at regular intervals so that employees and visitors can alert security if they need to.

A number of trash cans in the area have been removed and signs erected asking people to take their trash home with them. Ground staff check the area to make sure that it is litter free.

5. Perimeter Security

Check out your perimeter physical security systems – are they adequate?

Several areas of the perimeter were unlit at night.

Lighting and close circuit cameras have been installed with their own uninterruptible power supply.

The cameras are linked to a central control room manned 24/7 and they respond automatically to perimeter alarm events.

All access points into the facility are manned and all vehicles without parking decals are stopped and checked.

6. Building Usage

Must Do

It is essential to know everything about your building, who uses it, the main access points, traffic flow , different security levels, portals and so on.

There were eight unprotected access points into the building and no restrictions of movements within. There are now two main access points.

There is card reader access for employees at one entrance and visitors have to use the other and report to a security desk where they are logged in and issued name badges.

The building houses our company's headquarters and there are three other tenants. The tenants each have one floor of the building. Two of the tenants are administrative divisions of their respective companies, the third tenant is an internet service provider with a number of government clients and it houses all its main servers on its floor of the building. This area has been designated a high security, high risk area because of the confidential data stored there and the whole floor is protected by access devices, cameras and alarms to prevent unauthorized access. Portal protection between the different security tiers is considered adequate.

All stairwells are monitored by security cameras.

The mail room which was close to the lobby has been moved to a more secure area and can be immediately isolated in the event of an incident.

Safe rooms have been established throughout the building.

Critical Infrastructure

State and municipal governments across the country continue to take important steps to identify and assess the protection of key assets and services within their jurisdictions. Federal departments and agencies are working closely with industry to take stock of key assets and facilitate protective actions, while improving the timely exchange of important security related information.

Since implementation of the National Strategy for the Physical Protection of Critical Infrastructure and Key Assets The White House, 2003), the critical infrastructure sectors—those infrastructures and assets deemed most critical to national public health and safety, governance, economic and national security, and retaining public confidence—have been refined and expanded.

Critical infrastructure now includes:

* Agriculture.
* Banking and finance.
* Chemical and hazardous waste.
* Defense industrial base.
* Energy
* Transportation.
* Postal and shipping services.
* Public health.
* Water

Key assets now include:

* National monuments and icons.
* Nuclear power plants.
* Dams.
* Government facilities.
* Commercial assets.

7. Building Structure

Consult with your experts to determine if the building structure is safe or if physical hardening is needed.

Must Do

Two external walls which were closest to the road have been physically hardened and strengthened glass has been used in all windows.

A structural analysis has been performed and it has been determined that the walls could withstand the blast of either an internal or external bomb blast.

The floor, walls and ceiling of the mailing room have been reinforced in the event of an explosion.

The loading dock area has also been strengthened in order to withstand and contain an explosion.

8. Utility Systems

Utility systems are critical but often overlooked. You must know what utilities are used, how they enter the building, where they are vulnerable, is there onsite storage, back-up systems and so on.

Must Do

All utility inlets have been identified and protected. Some utility lines that were exposed above ground have been buried in armored cabling.

A utilities map has been prepared showing all the different utilities used – water, gas, electricity, telecoms etc - how they come on to the property, their pipelines or cables while on property and where they exit the property. It also shows all manholes, inspection points, sewer lines and so on. It also shows where water is stored on property, the source of water for the fire suppression system, the location of all electric service points and additional storage sites for other fuels.

Two manhole covers close to the company's car park are now padlocked.

All sprinkler and standpipe connections are inspected regularly.

A new, larger electrical generator has been acquired for emergency power. It is automatically activated in the event of an outage and it has its own supply of fuel – enough to last for 72 hours.

A transformer and switching gear outside the main building, which was easily accessible, is now encased in protective, secure and alarmed housing.

The electrical room has also been secured with controlled access and alarms.

The fire alarm system which was reliant on external communications, is now integrated within the IPS but has its own built in redundancies.

Fire dampers have been installed at all fire barriers.

All elevators can be individually or collectively isolated and shut down.

External air vents, which were accessible to the public, have been re-sited so that they are now inaccessible.

Air monitoring sensors have been introduced throughout the building and different sections of the HVAC system can be shut down and isolated as necessary.

Smoke evacuation systems have been installed.

Access to the roof is now controlled by keypad locks.

9. People

Must Do

In almost all cases people are your most critical asset, whether they are employees, tenants or visitors. You must know who uses the building and when, how they access and exit it, where they go when they are inside and whether their movement is controlled. You must also know what procedures are in place to screen staff and to train them in the event of an emergency. Even when you are just talking about implementing these measures, people feel more secure.

We have met with HR, tenants and others in order to come up with an accurate picture of exactly who uses our buildings, the times when most people arrive and leave and main traffic flows within the building.

We know when our deliveries are scheduled and who delivers them. (Note: a facilities manager admitted recently that while they employed an outside janitorial service, he had no idea who was on the cleaning crews with access to the most sensitive parts of the building. He also didn't know who was sent by the utilities companies to read meters and what supervision was in force when they were in the building.)

We have conducted studies to identify traffic flows – both vehicles and people – around the building.

All employees go through rigorous background checks.

People feel secure.

We have instituted a badge ID system for all regular building users with access controls at all entrances.

We have identified a number of different security layers/tiers within the facility and taken the appropriate steps to limit access to authorized personnel at access portals.

All visitors to the facility have to report to the front desk where their identities are established and the nature of their business at the facility confirmed. Bags are searched and they have to walk through a metal detector to gain access to the building. They are then issued a visitor's badge which has to be worn at all times while in the facility. The time of their arrival is logged as is their time of departure when they hand in the badge.

We have a team of security personnel, all carefully screened prior to hiring and all undergoing continuing on job training. They man the front desk, the security room which monitors CCTV and alarm/sensor control panels, and patrol the facility, both inside and out.

We have instituted a series of regular meetings with all employees to discuss security issues and the important part they play as our "eyes and ears". We believe that all our employees understand the need for security and the role they play in it.

Our IPS and emergency management plan are reviewed regularly and all safety, fire and evacuation drills are practiced on a regular basis.

10. Communications and IT

A key element of your integrated physical security plan is the protection of your IT, communications and information systems. Even though communications is a critical part of IPS, it is often covered in a separate plan. That is why integrated physical security is so important because it must incorporate all these separate threads into one cohesive and all encompassing plan.

Must Do

The main telephone distribution room has been made more secure and access to it is restricted and there is now an uninterruptible power supply and secure wiring.

We have also introduced redundant communications systems.

Access to the main IT control area is controlled and all back ups and tapes are stored in a fireproof safe and at a disaster recovery mirroring site.

We have also introduced a public address system so that everyone in the building can be alerted in the event of an emergency.

11. Equipment Operations & Maintenance

Must Do

You must know all about the equipment used in the building, how it operates and what the maintenance schedules are. Whenever you are discussing equipment needs there has to be an agreed level of redundancy, for instance, depending on the nature of the facility's mission, does it need one back up generator or two. If you do not know this information, make sure that the people who do have it are on your planning team.

All equipment, operations and maintenance manuals are regularly updated and are kept in a secure area.

All mechanical, electrical and plumbing systems are tested and balanced on a regular basis either by in-house maintenance staff or security screened sub-contractors.

Emergency lighting has been installed in all stair wells.

All back up systems are tested on a regular basis.

Level of redundancy is understood.

12. External Security Systems

Must Do

You must examine all your external security systems – are they adequate, are they integrated? Do they support your deter, detect and delay objectives?

Close circuit cameras have been installed around the perimeter linked to the control center that is manned 24/7. There is digital back up of all tapes.

The cameras have their own uninterrupted power supply.

The cameras have built in video motion capabilities.

Appropriate lighting. Lighting is not only an effective deterrent, it may well be essential for maximum functionality of your cameras.

Infrared sensors are located around the perimeter and the cameras respond automatically to perimeter alarm events.

Two intercom call boxes and improved lighting have been installed in the parking area. There are also panic/duress buttons appropriately positioned throughout the building.

Based on the advice of our consultants, a number of different sensor devices have been installed around the perimeter. These include active infrared, electromagnetic and microwave devices.

All vehicle traffic around the facility is monitored.

13. Internal Security Systems

As with external security systems above, you have to do a comprehensive evaluation of all internal security systems. Are they adequate for the job in hand, are there newer systems that could be implemented, are there areas that should be protected that are not currently covered?

Must Do

Close circuit cameras are used inside the facility and are monitored 24/7. Signals are transmitted by wireless and all images are backed up digitally.

All cameras are programmed to respond automatically to interior building alarm events.

There are now access control points at all entry points into the building.

Access controls have been implemented where different tiers of security have been identified.

All access control devices have an alternate power source in the event of an outage.

There are panic/duress alarm buttons and intercom call boxes strategically located throughout the building.

Metal detectors have been installed in the front lobby between the entrance and the security desk.

A number of different sensor systems have been installed throughout the building to detect intrusion.

A number of secure rooms have been established for the storage of sensitive information, valuable and/or potentially dangerous materials.

New security procedures have been introduced for handling mail and all potentially hazardous materials are now kept in a safe and secure area.

14. Security System Documents

Must Do An essential part of your IPS is to ensure that all security system documents are kept up to date, kept in a secure environment yet are available to the proper authorities in the event of an emergency.

All security system drawings, plans and manuals are kept in a secure, protected area yet can be made readily available to first responders.

Security system construction documentation has been prepared and standardized.

Security equipment selection criteria have been developed.

Contingency plans have been developed and tested in table top exercises.

Qualification guidelines have been determined for security consultants, system designers, engineers, installation vendors and contractors.

15. Security Master Plan

Must Do As with your security system documents, you have to ensure that your security master plan is regularly reviewed and revised to accommodate changing circumstances and new threats. It should be a constantly evolving and improving document.

There is a written system security plan for the building. It is regularly reviewed and revised as needed.

The plan has also been distributed to key management internally and to organizations and companies in the same field in order to develop benchmark guidelines and best practices.

The plan has been tested and evaluated from a benefit/cost and operational efficiency/ effective perspectives.

The plan meets all goals for protecting people, property, critical assets and information.

The plan meets all deter, detect, and delay criteria.

The plan meets all issues identified by the asset, threat, vulnerability and risk assessments.

The plan continues to meet all our short, medium and long term physical security goals and objectives.

16. Compliance

You must ensure that all modifications comply with all relevant codes.

Must Do

We have carried out our own inspections and have confirmed from all appropriate authorities that we are in full compliance.

Summary

Now that you have developed your model facility you can move on the next step. Your model facility is what you should have in a perfect world – how does that compare with your current situation? Welcome to Gap Analysis.

Step Two: Gap Analysis

Introduction

The goal of this phase is to identify the gaps between the model facility and your current situation. Before you can implement an integrated physical protection system, you have to know what you are protecting, who your adversaries are, what your critical assets are and the various systems and procedures you are going to use to prevent or mitigate them. You achieve this by carrying out a series of assessments and analyses to determine asset value and identify vulnerabilities, threats and probabilities of attack.

Must Do

Facility Mission & Critical Assets

First, however, you must be absolutely clear about the exact nature of your facility – what is its main mission or function and what are your critical assets – those things that are absolutely essential for performing that mission. Critical assets can be people, equipment, systems and processes or a combination of any or all of these.

Must Do

For instance, a school's main function is to teach and its critical assets are the teachers and students. Also important are the computers and other teaching aids that are used as well as the ancillary staff – but these are not as important as the teachers themselves. So you have to not only identify your critical assets you have to prioritize them as well.

Whatever type of facility you have, you must identify the key functions and all subsidiary functions and then identify the critical assets that are essential for maintaining and sustaining those functions. How would your ability to stay in businesses be impacted if, in the event of an attack, your critical assets were damaged or destroyed? How readily could these assets be replaced? Could they be replaced?

These are the questions you have to ask yourself and so before we can address threats and vulnerabilities, you have to identify your facility's mission and its critical assets.

Critical assets can generally be divided into the following groups:

☐ People

☐ Operations

☐ Information

Interdependencies

People

Remember

What is the building use and mix i.e. a multi-storey building might consist of an underground car park, shops on the first floor, offices on the next few floors and apartments on the top floors. How do people access the building? How many people are employed and what do they do, how many visitors are there on a daily basis? Are staff background checks carried out? Do you have security staff, how are they trained, are security procedures updated and practiced at regular intervals? Has the staff bought into the need for the upgraded security?

Map what different people do, where they go inside the building and how they get there. This will identify main traffic flows and how close they get to sensitive areas and critical assets. Do measures need to be introduced to redirect this traffic flow or do the sensitive areas need greater protection? Are certain parts of the building off-limits to some people and if so, how is access controlled and monitored? Are there different layers of security within the facility and if so, how is this the interface between the different levels (door, turnstile etc.) controlled?

Must Do

You must understand the traffic flow to, within and around your facility. This flow includes both people and vehicles. How many people and vehicles access your site, where do they gain access? Who uses the site and how can they be categorized – staff, visitors, delivery people, contractors and so on.

Do you provide parking facilities; can vehicles park on the street outside close to the building? You need to have to have this information in order to work out flow charts. This will show you which access points and doors are most used, any critical areas that are close to vehicle or people traffic and so on.

Operations

This covers all operations within the facility including security and safety – the day to day running of the building, shifts and shift changes, operating and operational procedures, equipment, maintenance, parking, deliveries and so on.

Information

Information covers internal matters such as in-house communications, protecting networks and sensitive documents, making sure that security staff and employees know what is happening, keeping documents and plans up to date. External issues include communications with all outside stakeholders (police, fire, local officials etc.), defending against cyber attack and ensuring that the appropriate authorities have access to documents and plans of your facility in the event of a major incident.

Interdependency

You cannot secure your building in isolation. You have to take into account upstream and downstream – what happens to shipments and materials before they enter your facility and after they have left and what is happening around you. You must consider your relationship with your neighbors and other facilities that might impact on you if they are attacked; your relationships with first responders and the wider community. While often overlooked, your insurance company is a key player and may be willing to assist with the implementation of a physical security plan if it reduces their liability in the event of an incident.

Remember

You must identify and assess all the risks, threats and vulnerabilities associated with each element, prioritize them and then decide on the best method of reducing or eliminating those threats. You must also take into account the often complex relationship between the various elements.

Must Do

Asset Value Assessment

An asset is a resource of value requiring protection. An asset can be tangible (e.g., tenants, buildings, facilities, equipment, activities, operations, and information) or intangible (e.g., processes or a company's reputation). In order to achieve the greatest risk reduction at the least cost, identifying and prioritizing a building's critical assets is vital in the process to identify the best mitigation measures to improve its level of protection prior to a terrorist attack. Recognizing that people are a building's most critical asset, the process described below will help identify and prioritize infrastructure where people are most at risk and require protection.

Define and understand the building's core functions and processes

☐ What are the building's primary services or outputs?

☐ What critical activities take place at the building?

☐ Who are the building's occupants and visitors?

☐ What inputs from external organizations are required for a building's success?

Identify building infrastructure

After the core functions and processes are identified, an evaluation of building infrastructure is the next step. To help identify and value rank infrastructure, the following should be considered, keeping in mind that the most vital asset for every building is its people:

Remember

☐ Identify how many people may be injured or killed during an incident that directly affects the infrastructure.

☐ Identify what happens to building functions, services, or occupant satisfaction if a specific asset is lost or degraded. (Can primary services continue?)

☐ Determine the impact on other organizational assets if the component is lost or can not function.

☐ Determine if critical or sensitive information is stored or handled at the building.

☐ Determine if backups exist for the building's assets.

- ☐ Determine the availability of replacements.
- ☐ Determine the potential for injuries or deaths from any catastrophic event at the building's assets.
- ☐ Identify any critical building personnel whose loss would degrade, or seriously complicate the safety of building occupants during an emergency.
- ☐ Determine if the building's assets can be replaced and identify replacement costs if the building is lost.
- ☐ Identify critical components/assets
- ☐ Security systems
- ☐ Identify the locations of key equipment.
- ☐ Life safety systems and safe haven areas
- ☐ Determine the locations of personnel work areas and systems.
- ☐ Identify the locations of any personnel operating "outside" a building's controlled areas.
- ☐ Determine, in detail, the physical locations of critical support architectures:
- ☐ Communications and information technology (IT - the flow of critical information and data)
- ☐ Utilities (e.g., facility power, water, air conditioning, etc.)
- ☐ Lines of communication that provide access to external resources and provide movement of people (e.g., road, rail, air transportation)
- ☐ Determine the location, availability, and readiness condition of emergency response assets, and the state of training of building staff in their use.

Cloud Computing and Outsourcing Data Storage

One of the biggest IT trends in the last few years has been the shift by major enterprises to cloud computing. Industry has increasingly become data dependent and constantly requires more space to house it. Data storage has gone from discs to servers, from closets to rooms, and from entire floors to complete buildings. It now makes much more sense - from an economic, strategic and security standpoint – to outsource this function.

Cloud computing customers do not own their own physical infrastructure – with huge savings in capital expenditure - but rent secure usage from a third-party provider. This way they don't have their own maintenance and storage costs and only pay for the resources that they use. Sharing services among many users also brings its own economies of scale for the service provider.

For the company it means considerable savings in hardware, software, maintenance and operating costs but the fact that it is now reliant on a third party provider also brings its own security challenges that have to be addressed as part of the Integrated Physical Security process.

There may be concerns about loss of control over sensitive data or information being accessed by people not unauthorized to do so. Securing and controlling the flow of this information and those who have access to it becomes even more difficult when thousands of employees might be located at destinations around the world and have access to it.

By requiring employees to log in to access information can also raise privacy issues because the company – and the provider – are able to monitor all user activity. Many experts believe that concerns over cloud computing security are delaying wider adoption.

These security issues involve both the service provider and the customer. The provider has the onus to ensure the infrastructure is secure and that client's data and applications are protected. The customer has the responsibility to check out the provider to satisfy themselves that the proper security measures are in place.

Issues to be considered by the client include: is the physical hardware secure; is the data secure, can it only be accessed by authorized users; can data privacy be maintained; is there an identity management system in place to control access to the information; and can authorized personnel access that data whenever they need to?

On the plus side, cloud computing increases reliability through the use of multiple redundant sites which makes it eminently suitable for business continuity and disaster recovery.

Critical Asset Worksheet #1 Sample

CRITICAL ASSET WORKSHEET #1 SAMPLE

| Objective: | Identify mission critical assets that allow you to operate and must be protected |
| Book Step : | Step 2 - Gap Analysis |

Purpose: The 1st phase in analyzing your security gaps / vulnerabilities is to identify the critical assets that must be protected. This chart will capture assets critical to your facility's mission & services provided to your customers

1. Action   Question: What is your facility's mission and what are the key services you provide ?
Answer :_____

2. Action

A - Document in the Asset Chart bellow your critical assets in 4 categories :
               People, Operations, Information & Interdependencies
B - Evaluate if there is a backup for this asset
C - Identify criticality of this asset (now that you know if there is a backup system)
            1 - Non critical, no major impact to facility mission if asset is taken out
            5 - Reversible impact, with cost & operational impacts
            10 - Non reversible and major impact to facility mission
D - Action Threshold : As a team, identify what assets will need to be protected (for example items ranked 5 & above)
Note - the items ranked Yes (Y), will be further developed in the Work Sheet #3 :   Facility Assessment Diagram

Example

A Asset Type	B Redundant sys / Backup?	C Criticality / Priority (1-10)	D Above threshold Y/N
People			
- Employees	No	10	Yes
Operations			
- Utilities: Power	Yes (Generator)	3	No
- Utilities: Water	No	5	Yes
Information			
- SCADA	No	10	Yes
- Confidential Financial info	Yes - Tape Backup	3	No
Interdependencies			
- Critical services from others	Yes - Other suppliers	3	No

Objective:

To identify critical assets that allow you to operate and which must be protected.

See the end of Step Two for a sample of a completed Critical Asset Worksheet and the end of the book for a blank worksheet that you can use.

Quantifying Critical Asset Value

Remember

After a building's assets or resources of value requiring protection have been identified, they should be assigned a value. Asset value is the degree of debilitating impact that would be caused by the incapacity or destruction of the building's assets. It is important to create an asset value so that you can prioritize them. Obviously, the key asset for most building is its people (e.g., employees, visitors, etc.) and they will always be assigned the highest asset value. There are a number of ways to assign an asset value and the example below uses a rating of 1-10.

Asset Value	
Very High	10
High	8-9
Medium High	7
Medium	5-6
Medium Low	4
Low	2-3
Very Low	1

Source: FEMA

- ☐ **Very High** - Loss or damage of the building's assets would have exceptionally grave consequences, such as extensive loss of life, widespread severe injuries, or total loss of primary services, core processes, and functions.

- ☐ **High** - Loss or damage of the building's assets would have grave consequences, such as loss of life, severe injuries, loss of primary services, or major loss of core processes and functions for an extended period of time.

- ☐ **Medium High** - Loss or damage of the building's assets would have serious consequences, such as serious injuries or impairment of core processes and functions for an extended period of time.

- ☐ **Medium** - Loss or damage of the building's assets would have moderate to serious consequences, such as injuries or impairment of core functions and processes.

- ☐ **Medium Low** - Loss or damage of the building's assets would have moderate consequences, such as minor injuries or minor impairment of core functions and processes.

- ☐ **Low** - Loss or damage of the building's assets would have minor consequences or impact, such as a slight impact on core functions and processes for a short period of time.

- ☐ **Very Low** - Loss or damage of the building's assets would have negligible consequences or impact.

Alternatively you can simply categorize your critical assets by assessing them a low, medium or high critical rating.

Identifying Threats

Now you know what you are protecting, you must identify what threats you face and where these threats might come from. This means identifying all internal and external threats and hazards and understanding why they might attack you. If you are in a high profile industry, you could be a target for terrorism; if you handle sensitive data you could be the victim of a cyber attack and if you sell jewelry or pharmaceuticals you might be burgled. The threat could also come from inside – violence or sabotage by a disgruntled employee or theft.

Fused Intelligence

The intelligence process is the foundation of threat assessment. Systematic exploitation of crime-related information can lead to and support evaluation and analysis of terrorism and terrorist groups. The who, what and where, when, how and motivation of terrorist groups are closely related. Intelligence efforts help produce reliable, informed responses to these questions. Without such a process, threat assessments can be unpredictable and unreliable.

You need to know who the bad buys are. This is done in a number of ways. You conduct a design basis threat assessment, and you consult with your local police, FBI and security consultants and you do "what if" scenario based assessments to cover every conceivable eventuality.

☐ **Asset Value** While the tragic events of 9/11 showed how vulnerable we were to attack – from either foreign or domestic terrorist groups, you will need to protect your facility from many other threats both internal and external. These include everything from internal pilfering to violence from a disgruntled employee to external threats such as theft, trespass, industrial espionage, natural disasters and terrorism. When you have identified your various adversaries, you can determine the probability of attack and the degree of threat that each one poses. Recent information gathered by intelligence and law enforcement agencies has led government officials to believe that both foreign and domestic terrorist groups continue to pose threats to the security of our nation's infrastructure, including our public buildings.

☐ **Asset Value** Your facility may not be a likely target for a terrorist attack but it may be in a high profile area where any attack will attract widespread publicity – a major aim of terrorism. You may be a soft target i.e. while your facility may not carry out a critical function, it may be an easier hit than the hard target up the road which has state of the art security in place.

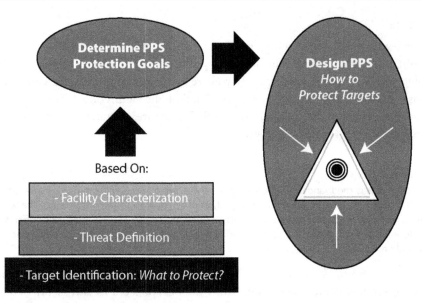

Information You Need to Define Threat

☐ Type of adversary: Terrorist, activist, employee, other

☐ Category of adversary: Foreign or domestic, terrorist or criminal, insider and/or outsider of the organization

☐ Objective of each type of adversary: Theft, sabotage, mass destruction (maximum casualties), sociopolitical statement, other

☐ Number of adversaries expected for each category: Individual suicide bomber, grouping or "cells" of operatives/terrorists, gangs, other

☐ Target selected by adversaries: Critical infrastructure, governmental buildings, national monuments, other

☐ Type of planning activities required to accomplish the objective: Longterm "casing," photography, monitoring police and security patrol patterns, other

☐ Most likely or "worst case" time an adversary could attack: When facility/location is fully staffed, at rush hour, at night, other

☐ Range of adversary tactics: Stealth, force, deceit, combination, other

☐ Capabilities of adversary: Knowledge, motivation, skills, weapons and tools.

One way to identify threats and where they could come from is to conduct a Design Basis Threat analysis.

Design Basis Threat (DBT)

DBT was originally developed to protect the nation's nuclear industry but the principles can be applied to any facility that needs to implement a physical security plan. Whether you are building a new facility or retrofitting an existing one, DBT helps you identify all your likely adversaries, lists their strengths and capabilities, what their targets might be, the likelihood of them attacking you and if so, how. When you have answered these questions and identified all threats, you are better able to design and incorporate safeguards to protect your facility and its critical assets. Consult local law enforcement, the FBI, Department of Homeland Security and other government agencies to help develop your DBT.

Tips

As an example, the nuclear industry is charged with doing design basis threat assessments to mitigate against threats equivalent to:

- ☐ the events of September 11, 2001
- ☐ a physical, cyber, biochemical, or other terrorist threat
- ☐ an attack on a facility by multiple coordinated teams of a large number of individuals
- ☐ assistance in an attack from several persons employed at the facility
- ☐ a suicide attack
- ☐ a water-based or air-based threat
- ☐ the use of explosive devices of considerable size and other modern weaponry
- ☐ an attack by persons with a sophisticated knowledge of the operations of a sensitive nuclear facility
- ☐ fire, especially a fire of long duration; and
- ☐ any other threat that the Nuclear Regulatory Commission determines should be included as an element of the design basis threat.

Your facility may not be as high-risk as a nuclear power plant, but the methodology used to identify adversaries, their motivations, their strengths, their capabilities and how they might attack you are just as applicable to your facility.

Design Basis Threat Worksheet #2 Sample

DESIGN BASIS THREAT WORKSHEET #2 SAMPLE

Objective:	Identify & document who you are protecting your facility against
Book Step :	Step 2 Gap Analysis

Purpose: The 2nd phase in analyzing your security vulnerabilities is to identify what you are protecting your facility against. This chart will capture who your potential adversaries are and what are their potential capabilities

Action 1: Data Gathering
In order to narrow your threats to the most realistic ones your 1st step would be a Data collection activity. There are several sources you will need to draw on – your local law enforcement (FBI, Sheriff etc.), Other similar type facilities, neighboring facilities etc.

Question Is there historical data that would identify potential threats to your facility?
Question Do the law enforcement authorities have specific intelligence that could narrow the list of potential threats?
Question Talk to similar facilities - are they aware of specific risks to your facility type?
Question Talk to your local community, neighbors - have there been any recent events that could indicate potential adversarial profiles?

Action 2: Develop your adversary list based on the above Data gathering
   A - List your potential adversaries
   B - What is their motive to execute their attack
   C - Profile of adversaries - how many, armed, on foot, equipped with hand tools
   D - Identify what is the realistic probability of an attack

Vulnerability
   Low - very slim chances
   Medium - could happen
   High - Highly probable

Note : Action 2D is critical because the core team will need to establish what adversaries to protect the facility against. A scenario based analysis will be done for each realistic adversary type and actions will be taken to protect the facility against these specific threats.
As a core team you will need to define the threshold for your DBT (for example Medium probability and above)

Example

	A	B	C	D		
	Adversary List/type	Motive	Profile/ Characteristics	Probability of Attack		
				Low	Medium	High
1	Insider	Disgruntled Employee	Alone, has access to critical assets			H
2	Vandal	Just for Kicks	Adolescent group of 3 to 5		M	
3	Terrorist	Media, sent on a mission	Alone, suicide bomber	L		

Objective:

Identify who you are protecting your facility against.

See the end of Step Two for a sample of a completed Design Basis Threat Worksheet and the end of the book for a blank worksheet that you can use.

Note: It, hopefully, goes without saying but all these documents should be kept secure!

The important thing is that assessment is not a one off process. It is not just one of the steps involved in the development of your physical protection plan, it is an ongoing process that must be kept under constant review. New or changed circumstances mean different scenarios will have to be analyzed and this may lead to changes or refinements in your physical security planning.

The Department of Defense has established the following threat categories. Security threats are classified as either human or natural. Human threats are carried out by a wide range of aggressors who may have one or more objectives toward assets such as equipment, personnel, and operations. Aggressors can be categorized and their objectives can be generalized as described below.

Aggressor Objectives

Four major objectives describe an aggressor's behavior. Any one of the first three objectives can be used to realize the fourth. These objectives include—

- ☐ Inflicting injury or death on people.
- ☐ Destroying or damaging facilities, property, equipment, or resources.
- ☐ Stealing equipment, materiel, or information.
- ☐ Creating adverse publicity.

Aggressor Categories

Aggressors are grouped into five broad categories—criminals, vandals and activists, extremists, protest groups, and terrorists. Hostile acts performed by these aggressors range from crimes (such as burglary) to low intensity conflict threats (such as unconventional warfare). Each of these categories describes predictable aggressors who pose threats to military assets and who share common objectives and tactics.

- ☐ Criminals can be characterized based on their degree of sophistication. They are classified as unsophisticated criminals, sophisticated criminals, and organized criminal groups. Their common objective is the theft of assets; however, the assets they target, the quantities they seek, their relative efficiency, and the sophistication of their actions vary significantly. Vandals and activists may also be included under this category.
- ☐ Vandals and activists are groups of protesters who are politically or issue oriented. They act out of frustration, discontent, or anger against the actions of other social or political groups. Their primary objectives commonly include destruction and publicity. Their selection of targets will vary based on the risk associated with attacking them. The degree of damage they seek to cause will vary with their sophistication.
- ☐ Extremists are radical in their political beliefs and may take extreme, violent actions to gain support for their beliefs or cause.
- ☐ Protesters are considered a threat only if they are violent. Lawful protesters have to be considered, but significant protective measures and procedures are not normally needed to control their actions. The presence of extremists or vandals/activists at a peaceful protest increases the chance of the protest becoming violent.

☐ Terrorists are ideologically, politically, or issue oriented. They commonly work in small, well-organized groups or cells. They are sophisticated, are skilled with tools and weapons, and possess an efficient planning capability. There are three types of terrorists— CONUS, OCONUS, and paramilitary OCONUS.

- CONUS terrorists are typically right- or left-wing extremists operating in distinct areas of the US.

- OCONUS terrorists generally are more organized than CONUS terrorists. They usually include ethnically or religiously oriented groups.

- Paramilitary OCONUS terrorist groups show some military capability with a broad range of military and improvised weapons.

- Attacks by OCONUS terrorists are typically more severe.

Natural threats are usually the consequence of natural phenomena. They are not preventable by physical-security measures, but they are likely to have significant effects on security systems and operations. They may require an increase in protective measures either to address new situations or to compensate for the loss of existing security measures. They may reduce the effectiveness of existing security measures by such occurrences as collapsed perimeter fences and barriers, inoperable protective lighting, damaged patrol vehicles, and poor visibility. Natural threats and their effects relative to security include the following:

☐ Floods may result in property damage, destruction of perimeter fences, and damage to IDSs. Heavy rains or snowfalls may have similar effects even if they do not result in flooding.

☐ Storms, tornadoes, high winds, or rain may cause nuisance alarms to activate and cause damage to IDSs. They may limit the visibility of security personnel and may affect close-circuit television (CCTV) systems. Winds may also disrupt power or communication lines and cause safety hazards from flying debris.

☐ Earthquakes may cause nuisance alarms to activate or may disrupt IDSs. They may also cause broken water or gas mains, fallen electrical or communication lines, and weakened or collapsed buildings.

☐ Snow and ice can make travel on patrol roads difficult, may delay responses to alarms, may impede the performance of IDSs, and may freeze locks and alarm mechanisms. Heavy ice may also damage power and communication lines.

☐ Fires may damage or destroy perimeter barriers and buildings, possibly leaving assets susceptible to damage or theft.

☐ Fog can reduce the visibility of security forces, thereby requiring additional security personnel. It may also increase the response time to alarms and reduce the effectiveness of security equipment such as CCTV systems.

Aggressor Tactics

Aggressors have historically used a wide range of offensive strategies reflecting their capabilities and objectives. They can be generally categorized as force, stealth and deceit. Separating these tactics into categories allows facility planners and physical-security personnel to define threats in standardized terms usable as a basis for facility and security-system design. Common aggressor tactics include—

- ☐ **Moving vehicle bomb.** An aggressor drives an explosive-laden car or truck into a facility and detonates the explosives. His goal is to damage or destroy the facility or to kill people. This is a suicide attack.

- ☐ **Stationary vehicle bomb.** An aggressor covertly parks an explosive laden car or truck near a facility. He then detonates the explosives either by time delay or remote control. His goal in this tactic is the same as for the moving vehicle bomb with the additional goal of destroying assets within the blast area. This is commonly not a suicide attack. It is the most frequent application of vehicle bombings.

- ☐ **Exterior attack.** An aggressor attacks a facility's exterior or an exposed asset at close range. He uses weapons such as rocks, clubs, improvised incendiary or explosive devices, and hand grenades. Weapons (such as small arms) are not included in this tactic, but are considered in subsequent tactics. His goal is to damage the facility, to injure or kill its occupants, or to damage or destroy assets.

- ☐ **Standoff weapons.** An aggressor fires military weapons or improvised versions of military weapons at a facility from a significant distance. These weapons include direct (such as antitank [AT] weapons) and indirect LOS weapons (such as mortars). His goal is to damage the facility, to injure or kill its occupants, or to damage or destroy assets.

- ☐ **Ballistics.** The aggressor fires various small arms (such as pistols, submachine guns, shotguns, and rifles) from a distance. His goal is to injure or kill facility occupants or to damage or destroy assets.

- ☐ **Forced entry.** The aggressor forcibly enters a facility using forced entry tools (such as hand, power, and thermal tools) and explosives. He uses the tools to create a man-passable opening or to operate a device in the facility's walls, doors, roof, windows, or utility openings. He may also use small arms to overpower guards. His goal is to steal or destroy assets, compromise information, injure or kill facility occupants, or disrupt operations.

- ☐ **Covert entry.** The aggressor attempts to enter a facility or a portion of a facility by using false credentials or stealth. He may try to carry weapons or explosives into the facility. His goals include those listed for forced entry.

- ☐ **Insider compromise.** A person authorized access to a facility (an insider) attempts to compromise assets by taking advantage of that accessibility. The aggressor may also try to carry weapons or explosives into the facility in this tactic. His goals are the same as those listed for forced entry.

☐ **Visual surveillance.** The aggressor uses ocular and photographic devices (such as binoculars and cameras with telephoto lenses) to monitor facility or installation operations or to see assets. His goal is to compromise information. As a precursor, he uses this tactic to determine information about the asset of interest.

☐ **Acoustic eavesdropping.** The aggressor uses listening devices to monitor voice communications or other audibly transmitted information. His goal is to compromise information.

☐ **Electronic-emanations eavesdropping.** The aggressor uses electronic-emanation surveillance equipment from outside a facility or its restricted area to monitor electronic emanations from computers, communications, and related equipment. His goal is to compromise information.

☐ **Mail-bomb delivery.** The aggressor delivers bombs or incendiary devices to the target in letters or packages. The bomb sizes involved are relatively small. His goal is to kill or injure people.

☐ **Supplies-bomb delivery.** The aggressor conceals bombs in various containers and delivers them to supply- and material-handling points such as loading docks. The bomb sizes in this tactic can be significantly larger that those in mail bombs. His goal is to damage the facility, kill or injure its occupants, or damage or destroy assets.

☐ **Airborne contamination.** An aggressor contaminates a facility's air supply by introducing chemical or biological agents into it. His goal is to kill or injure people.

☐ **Waterborne contamination.** An aggressor contaminates a facility's water supply by introducing chemical, biological, or radiological agents into it. These agents can be introduced into the system at any location with varying effects, depending on the quantity of water and the contaminant involved. His goal is to kill or injure people.

The aforementioned tactics are typical threats to fixed facilities for which designers and physical-security personnel can provide protective measures. However, some common terrorist acts are beyond the protection that facility designers can provide. They cannot control kidnappings, hijackings, and assassinations that take place away from facilities or during travel between facilities. Protection against these threats is provided through operational security and personal measures.

Remember It is very difficult to stop a determined terrorist attack on a building. However, the more secure the building or site and the better the building is designed to withstand an attack, the better the odds the building will not be attacked or, if attacked, will suffer less damage.

Terrorists generally select targets that have some value as a target, such as an iconic commercial property, symbolic government building, or structure likely to inflict significant emotional or economic damage such as a shopping mall or major seaport.

A manmade threat/hazard analysis requires interface with security and intelligence organizations that understand the locality, the region, and the nation. These organizations include the police department (whose jurisdiction includes the building or site), the local state police office, and the local office of the FBI. In many areas of the country, there are threat coordinating committees, including FBI Joint Terrorism Task Forces, that facilitate the sharing of information.

Terrorist Threat Evaluation

A common method to evaluate terrorist threats is to analyze five factors: existence, capability, history, intention, and targeting.

☐ **Existence addresses the questions:** Who is hostile to the assets, organization, or community of concern? Are they present or thought to be present? Are they able to enter the country or are they readily identifiable in a local community upon arrival?

☐ **Capability addresses the questions:** What weapons have been used in carrying out past attacks? Do the aggressors need to bring them into the area or are they available locally?

☐ **History addresses the questions:** What has the potential threat element done in the past and how many times? When was the most recent incident and where, and against what target? What tactics did they use? Are they supported by another group or individuals? How did they acquire their demonstrated capability?

☐ **Intention addresses the questions:** What does the potential threat element or aggressor hope to achieve? How do we know this (e.g., published in books or news accounts, speeches, letters to the editor, informant)?

☐ **Targeting addresses the questions:** Do we know if an aggressor (we may not know which specific one) is performing surveillance on our building, nearby buildings, or buildings that have much in common with our organization? Is this information current and credible, and indicative of preparations for terrorist operations (manmade hazards)?

Sources of threat information

www.ready.gov	Department of Homeland Defense
www.infragard.net	Threat notices and bulletins
www.state.gov/travel	Dept of State travel warnings
www.whitehouse.gov/homeland	Homeland Security
www.asisonline.org	American Society of Industrial Security
www.securitymanagement.com	ASIS magazine
www.twotigersonline.com/resources.html	Private web site on Homeland Defense

www.fbi.gov	FBI
www.usdoj.gov	Dept of Justice
www.state.gov	Dept of State
www.janes.com	Jane's Information Group
www.defendamerica.mil	DoD news on terrorism
www.dhs.gov	Dept of Homeland Security
www.nipc.gov	National Infrastructure Protection Center

Another valuable tool is Crime Prevention Through Environmental Design (CPTED)

CPTED is a crime prevention approach that has been developed successfully over many years and takes into account the relationship between the physical environment and the users of that environment. By talking to local law enforcement you can identify the sort of crimes that occur in the vicinity of your facility and gather information about likely perpetrators.

Vulnerability Assessment

Having identified your critical assets and who might attack them, you now have to determine how vulnerable those assets are to attack. How effective is your existing security? Do you have any physical security in place? Conduct a security inventory based on the master assessment checklist.

Checklist

What is your current security situation ?

☐ Are you at risk from your neighbors?

☐ How secure is your location?

☐ What is my current perimeter security?

☐ How structurally safe is my facility?

☐ Are my utilities safe and if so, how?

☐ What communications/IT protection do I have?

☐ Is my equipment protected?

☐ What external security protection do I have?

☐ What internal security protection do I have?

Remember the basic principles of physical security – deter, detect, delay and response (DDDR). Does your current physical security help achieve effective DDDR.

Note: There are many methodologies for conducting risk assessment and they may use different criteria. In deciding which methodology is best for you seek advice. For instance, some funding sources may require that a particular methodology is used, some methodologies may be more appropriate for your type of enterprise and so on.

Facility Vulnerability Assement Worksheet #3 Sample

FACILITY VULNERABILITY ASSESSMENT WORKSHEET #3 SAMPLE

Objective: Diagram the existing site conditions, noting critical assets (from WS #1 column D) & existing security systems.
Book Step : Step 2 - Gap Analysis

Purpose: The 3rd phase in analyzing your security situation is to document where the critical assets are on site and what
security systems exist.
This diagram will be used to develop a scenario based analysis of how an asset could be compromised.
In other words what are the security vulnerabilities that will need to be addressed & mitigated in the future.

Action1. Sketch a diagram of your facility including your site   (your goal is to show minimal information necessary not maximum detail)
Show major amenities, buildings, roads, parking, site neighbors,
Show existing security components/ sytems: fencing, guardhouse, lighting, CCTV etc.

Action 2. Locate and draw in the critical assets identified in WS #1   (ones that are above the acceptable threshold)
Draw a legend for the graphics you developed on your diagram.

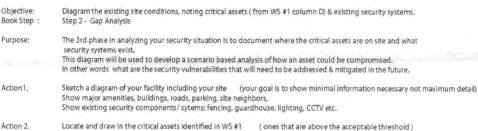

Objective:

To identify where your critical assets are and how they are currently protected.

See the end of Step Two for a sample of a completed Vulnerability Assessment Worksheet and the end of the book for a blank worksheet that you can use.

Major steps in conducting a vulnerability assessment

☐ Characterize facility

☐ Identify Assets or "targets" and Consequence of loss

☐ Identify credible Threats against assets

☐ Analyze undesired events

☐ Analyze likelihood of occurrence

☐ Consequence of loss

☐ Evaluate ranked list of vulnerabilities

☐ Impact on facility mission – low, medium, high

Determining the Vulnerability Rating

This task involves determining a vulnerability rating that reflects the weakness of functions, systems, and sites in regard to a particular threat. Weakness includes the lack of redundancies that will make the building system operational after an attack.

Redundancy Factor

A terrorist selects the weapon and tactic that will cause harm to people, destroy the infrastructure, or functionally defeat the target. The function and infrastructure vulnerability analysis will identify the geographic distribution within the building and interdependencies between critical assets. Ideally, the functions should have geographic dispersion as well as a recovery site or alternate work location. However, some critical functions and infrastructure do not have a backup, or will be determined to be collocated and create what are called single-point vulnerabilities. Identification and protection of these single-point vulnerabilities is a key aspect of the assessment process. Concerns related to common system vulnerabilities are:

☐ No redundancy

☐ Redundant systems feed into single critical node

☐ Critical components of redundant systems collocated

☐ Inadequate capacity or endurance in post-attack environment

☐ Identification and protection of these single-point vulnerabilities will help you to determine a more accurate vulnerability rating for your assessment.

The following chart illustrates system vulnerabilities and how redundancies should be built in.

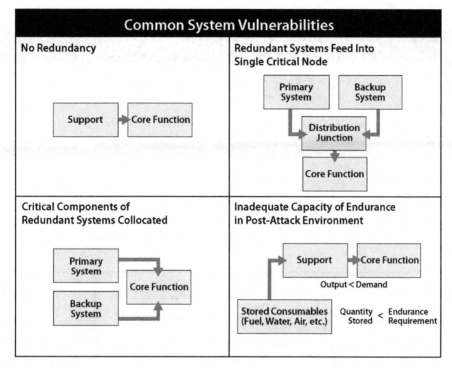

Source: FEMA

Scenario Assessment Worksheet #4 Sample

SCENARIO ASSESSMENT WORKSHEET #4 SAMPLE

Objective:	Identify facility security vulnerabilities per adversary scenario
Book Step :	Step 2 - Gap Analysis

Purpose: The 4th phase in analyzing your security situation is to find the flaws that would allow an adversary to attack & compromise your critical assets.
Using the facility diagram you created (WS #3), a scenario based analysis will take place in which you will look at ways a chosen adversary would obtain access to the facility and attack the critical assets.

Action 1.   Map out how your adversary will attack your facility
A - Identify the route, the means & what would allow your adversary to achieve his goal.

Action 2.   B - Identify what systems will allow the adversary to enter & achieve his goal:
Unprotected windows, poor hardware on gate, password on computer written on sticky note... etc.
These are the facility Security Vulnerabilities

C - List the type of system that failed to detect, delay, assess or respond to these scenario based adversaries actions.

Scenario: 1   Adversary: Disgruntled Employee

Example

A Adversary Attack/ Vulnerability	B Allowing Systems - Vulnerabilities	C Type of System
Insider has card access to site, enters site during off hours, enters the SCADA room with card.	One card access system - allows access to all employees to all rooms on campus 24/7. There is no way to detect entry to critical areas on site	Physical / Operational
Access to computer system by using password on sticky-note posted on monitor.	Passwords are not personal & not protected,	Policy
Next day multiple system disruptions, take down the entire sytem .	Lack of redundancy / no backup systems	Operations
Lack of a back up system resulted in loss of product to core clients	Employee not flagged as a threat	Operations
During the entire event, no one knew about the breach and there would be no one trained to respond	To date there has been no training to respond to breach of access contol at this facility	Operations

Objective:

To identify flaws in your current security situation that make you vulnerable.

See the end of Step Two for a sample of a completed Critical Asset Worksheet and the end of the book for a blank worksheet that you can use.

Once vulnerabilities have been identified, they also need to be rated so that you can prioritize them as the following examples illustrate.

Vulnerability Rating

Criteria		
Very High	10	Very High – One or more major weaknesses have been identified that make the asset extremely susceptible to an aggressor or hazard. The building lacks redundancies/physical protection and the entire building would be only functional again after a very long period of time after the attack.
High	8-9	High – One or more major weaknesses have been identified that make the asset highly susceptible to an aggressor or hazard. The building has poor redundancies/physical protection and most parts of the building would be only functional again after a long period of time after the attack.
Medium High	7	Medium High – An important weakness has been identified that makes the asset very susceptible to an aggressor or hazard. The building has inadequate redundancies/physical protection and most critical functions would be only operational again after a long period of time after the attack.
Medium	5-6	Medium – A weakness has been identified that makes the asset fairly susceptible to an aggressor or hazard. The building has insufficient redundancies/physical protection and most part of the building would be only functional again after a considerable period of time after the attack.
Medium Low	4	Medium Low – A weakness has been identified that makes the asset somewhat susceptible to an aggressor or hazard. The building has incorporated a fair level of redundancies/physical protection and most critical functions would be only operational again after a considerable period of time after the attack.
Low	2-3	Low – A minor weakness has been identified that slightly increases the susceptibility of the asset to an aggressor or hazard. The building has incorporated a good level of redundancies/physical protection and the building would be operational within a short period of time after an attack.
Very Low	1	Very Low – No weaknesses exist. The building has incorporated excellent redundancies/physical protection and the building would be operational immediately after an attack.

Source: FEMA

Nominal Example of Threat Rating for an Urban Multi-story Building (Building Function)

Function	Cyber Attack	Vehicle Bomb	Suicide Bomber	Chemical (Sarin)	Biological
Administration	8	4	5	2	2
Engineering	8	4	5	2	2
Warehousing	8	4	5	2	2
Data Center	8	4	5	2	2
Food Service	8	4	5	2	2
Security	8	4	5	2	2
Housekeeping	8	4	5	2	2
Day Care	8	4	5	2	2

Nominal Example of Threat Rating for an Urban Multi-story Building (Building Infrastructure)

Infrastructure					
Site	8	4	5	2	2
Architectural	8	4	5	2	2
Structural Systems	8	4	5	2	2
Envelope Systems	8	4	5	2	2
Utility Systems	8	4	5	2	2
Mechanical Systems	8	4	5	2	2
Plumbing and Gas Systems	8	4	5	2	2
Electrical Systems	8	4	5	2	2
Fire Alarm Systems	8	4	5	2	2
IT/Communications Systems	8	4	5	2	2

Source: FEMA

Nominal Example of Threat Rating for an Urban Multi-story Building (Building Function)

Function	Cyber Attack	Vehicle Bomb	Suicide Bomber	Chemical (Sarin)	Biological
Administration	8	4	5	2	2
Engineering	8	4	5	2	2
Warehousing	8	4	5	2	2
Data Center	8	4	5	2	2
Food Service	8	4	5	2	2
Security	8	4	5	2	2
Housekeeping	8	4	5	2	2
Day Care	8	4	5	2	2

Nominal Example of Threat Rating for an Urban Multi-story Building (Building Infrastructure)

Infrastructure					
Site	8	4	5	2	2
Architectural	8	4	5	2	2
Structural Systems	8	4	5	2	2
Envelope Systems	8	4	5	2	2
Utility Systems	8	4	5	2	2
Mechanical Systems	8	4	5	2	2
Plumbing and Gas Systems	8	4	5	2	2
Electrical Systems	8	4	5	2	2
Fire Alarm Systems	8	4	5	2	2
IT/Communications Systems	8	4	5	2	2

Source: FEMA

Worksheet: Vulnerability Rating

WORKSHEET: Vulnerability Rating

Function	Vulnerability	Infrastructure	Vulnerability
Administration		Site	
Engineering		Architectural	
Warehousing		Structural Systems	
Data Center		Envelope Systems	
Food Service		Utility Systems	
Security		Mechanical Systems	
Housekeeping		Plumbing and Gas Systems	
Day Care		Electrical Systems	
Other		Fire Alarm Systems	
Other		IT/Communications Systems	

Source: FEMA

Facility Characterization

Characterize the facility in terms of:

☐ Site boundary

☐ Buildings (construction and HVAC systems)

☐ Room locations

☐ Access points

☐ Processes within the facility

☐ Operating conditions (working hours, off-hours, potential emergencies)

☐ Existing physical protection facilities

☐ Safety considerations

☐ Types and numbers of employees

These vulnerabilities or weaknesses identify areas that could be exploited by an aggressor. By identifying them you can incorporate specific physical security elements in your plan to mitigate them.

Remember

Is my perimeter secure enough to prevent a vehicle bomb from crashing through it? Are my confidential computer files safe from hackers? Can I control people and vehicle access to sensitive parts of the facility? Can I effectively isolate the mail room in the event of a biohazard parcel bomb explosion?

If vs. When

When planning, there are really two scenarios – if and when. The "if" scenario covers planning and procedures to prevent the likelihood of an incident and is concerned with deterrence, detection, delay and response and how each of these impacts our four key elements – people, operations, interdependency and information. The "when" scenario covers planning and procedures both during and after an incident and is mainly concerned with mitigation.

Vulnerabilities may include the siting of the building, its physical layout, inadequate security systems and ineffective security procedures and badly trained staff. Remember that you may also be vulnerable to weaknesses outside your immediate control. For instance, a plant producing toxic chemicals up the road may be the target for a terrorist attack but your building could be affected by the plume of poisonous gases swept your way, so you must plan accordingly.

Remember

One helpful way of identifying vulnerabilities is to conduct scenario based assessments. This is a very analytical process because you must be able to identify fatal flaws in your current situation, weakest points and so on. You have to come up with multiple "what if" scenarios and work them through. What would happen if a disgruntled employee walks into the facility armed with a gun? What would happen if a cyber terrorist steals highly sensitive data from your server? What would happen if the mailroom opened a packet releasing biologically hazardous material?

Tips

By working through the various scenarios and determining probable actions and consequences, you can then develop plans to counter or mitigate them.

One useful way to evaluate different types of facilities is to conduct a tier assessment. This is helpful in determining the nature of your facility and its risk level which allows you to prioritize your requirements. The following methodology was developed by the Department of Defense and is a good example of tier assessment.

Tier Assessments

While the fundamentals of integrated physical security apply to all buildings the degree of security required will depend on the nature of the facility. If you are a low-risk, non governmental administrative building your requirements will not be as great as a federal court house or other high-risk target.

Understanding Tiers

The level of the assessment for a given building is dependent upon a number of factors such as type of building, location, type of construction, number of occupants, economic life, and other owner specific concerns and available economic resources. The levels of the assessment provided are similar to the FEMA 310 process and provide increasing tiers of assessments. The underlying purpose is to provide a variable scale to meet benefit/cost considerations for a given building that meets the intent and requirements of available antiterrorism guidelines such as the DoD Minimum Antiterrorism Standards and the GSA Interagency Security Criteria.

☐ **Tier 1.** A Tier 1 assessment is a screening phase that identifies the primary vulnerabilities and mitigation options, and is a "70 percent" assessment. A Tier 1 assessment can typically be conducted by one or two experienced assessment professionals in approximately 2 days with the building owner and key staff; it involves a "quick look" at the site perimeter, building, core functions, infrastructure, drawings, and plans. A Tier 1 assessment will likely be sufficient for the majority of commercial buildings and other noncritical facilities and infrastructure.

☐ **Tier 2.** A Tier 2 assessment is a full on-site evaluation by assessment specialists that provides a robust evaluation of system interdependencies, vulnerabilities, and mitigation options; it is a "90 percent" assessment solution. A Tier 2 assessment typically requires three to five assessment specialists, can be completed in 3 to 5 days, and requires significant key building staff participation (e.g., providing access to all site and building areas, systems, and infrastructure) and an indepth review of building design documents, drawings, and plans. A Tier 2 assessment is likely to be sufficient for most high-risk buildings such as iconic commercial buildings, government facilities, schools, hospitals, and other designated high value infrastructure assets.

☐ **Tier 3**. A Tier 3 assessment is a detailed evaluation of the building using blast and weapons of mass destruction (WMD) models to determine building response, survivability, and recovery, and the development of mitigation options. A Tier 3 assessment typically involves engineering and scientific experts and requires detailed design information, including drawings and other building information. Modeling and analysis can often take several days or weeks and is typically performed for high value and critical infrastructure assets. The Assessment Team is not defined for this tier; however, it could be composed of 8 to 12 people.

Tier One Screening Phase

To prepare an effective assessment, the following activities should take place:

☐ **Pre-Meeting and Preparation of a Schedule and Tentative Agenda.** Before conducting the on-site building evaluation, a coordination meeting should take place. During this meeting, the type of assessment to be conducted, personnel availability, schedules, and outputs should be discussed in detail. In addition, firm timetables and an agenda for on-site visits should be discussed. The agenda schedule should include the sites to be evaluated and special areas to be protected.

☐ **On-Site Meeting(s).** For each assessment, a preparation meeting will take place with key stakeholders. Upon arrival at the site or building, the Team should have an introduction meeting with key staff, review the available information, and review the vulnerability portfolio. As a minimum, recommended building personnel attendees should include:

Checklist

☐ Site or building owner

☐ Chief of engineering

☐ Chief of security

☐ Chief of IT

☐ Emergency manager

Other attendees may include:

☐ Union or employee representatives

☐ Local law enforcement, fire, and EMS representatives

☐ State or county representatives

☐ Local utility, telecommunications, and services (waste, security services, etc.)

☐ Administration, food services, laboratory, and other critical function representatives

For the assessment to be successful, building stakeholders should participate as key members, providing on-site access to all buildings and areas. In addition, they should participate in interviews, and provide comments on current strengths and weakness of plans and procedures, including facility access, personnel movement, operations and maintenance, and security alerts.

Windshield Tour(s). After the introduction meeting, the Assessment Team and stakeholders should conduct a "windshield" tour or walk-around of the key facilities. The Assessment Team may find areas that require special attention and feel the need to make adjustments to the assessment agenda.

Tips

Assessment Background Information. After the on-site tour, the Assessment Team and stakeholders are ready to conduct the on-site assessment. Completing the matrices provided for conducting the threat assessment will take approximately 4 to 8 hours, using an interview and consensus approach around a table. During these discussions, the Team should prepare worksheets to determine:

- ☐ Threats that are a priority concern for your site, building, and related infrastructure
- ☐ The assets of your area, building or site that can be affected by a threat

Review Key Documents. The Assessment Team will review or evaluate a number of plans, procedures, and policies. The list below provides some of the documents that need to be reviewed by the Team before conducting the assessment.

Checklist

- ☐ Prior vulnerability assessment data
- ☐ Emergency response and disaster recovery plans
- ☐ Security master plan (including detection/delay/assess)
- ☐ Security inspection results
- ☐ HazMat plans
- ☐ Policy and legal requirements
- ☐ Federal, State, and local law enforcement threat assessments
- ☐ Site plans of utility and communications systems
- ☐ Floor plans for all facilities identified as important (including those listed above)
- ☐ Floor plans and locations of modified and abandoned facilities
- ☐ Structural drawings of key facilities
- ☐ New project drawings for fences, security, and buildings
- ☐ Security system drawings
- ☐ Historical reports
- ☐ Local zoning ordinances
- ☐ Comprehensive plans
- ☐ Development plans
- ☐ Information on the facility systems operations capability
- ☐ Information on agreements with the surrounding community and Federal agencies
- ☐ Information on incidents within the building (i.e., misconduct information)
- ☐ Population statistics
- ☐ Manpower surveys
- ☐ Other documents determined by the Team to be important

Review Emergency Procedures. The Assessment Team and building stakeholders should review the security master plan, and the engineering operations and maintenance, emergency operations, and disaster recovery plans to understand the critical assets of the building and establish a baseline organization response and recovery capability in case of an attack or event. The impact of many vulnerabilities can be reduced or eliminated by simple changes in plans, policies, and procedures. As part of the screening phase review, the following areas should be considered:

Emergency notification procedures

☐ Emergency evacuation procedures

☐ First responder access and routing

☐ Shelter-in-place procedures

☐ Designated shelter capacities and travel routes

☐ Off-site rally point and roll call

☐ Emergency engineering systems shutdown (HVAC, electrical, information technology (IT)/telecommunications)

☐ Portable protective equipment (indoor air filters, sampling kits, first aid)

☐ Personal protective equipment (PPE)

☐ Exercise of plans

Checklist

Prepare the Assessment. Preparing the assessment can be as simple as a quick review and analysis of existing documents and a short walk around the site, or a more detailed in-depth review and analysis of the documents, plans, and other information and a thorough walk-through of the building, including utility spaces, basements, crawl spaces, attics, and vault. The following are recommended when conducting the different types of assessments.

For Tier 1 Screening Evaluation, the analysis should include, at a minimum:

☐ Perimeter identification

☐ Vehicle and pedestrian entry access control points

☐ Security operations function

☐ EOC (or function)

☐ Primary point of entry of utilities and telecommunications

☐ Critical functions

☐ Critical infrastructure

☐ Key staff

☐ Off-site rally point and other Emergency Management procedures (PPE, mass notification, etc.)

For Tier 2 On-Site Evaluation, the analysis should include, at a minimum:

☐ Tier 1 information

☐ Detailed inspection and route tracing of primary utilities and telecommunications

☐ Detailed review of HVAC system and operating parameters

Checklist

- Detailed review of electric power and generator capacity (life safety, data centers, communications, etc.)
- Detailed review of structural and envelope system (column-beam connections, materials, clips, glazing)
- Detailed review of Security Master Plan, Emergency Management Plan, other related plans and Memorandums of Understanding (MOU) (Continuity of Operations [COOP], Continuity of Government [COG], Certified Emergency Management Plan [CEMP], etc.)

For Tier 3, Detailed Evaluation, the analysis should include, at a minimum:

- Tier 2 information
- Systems interdependencies on-site and off-site (utility vaults, communications central office trunks, transportation nodes, logistics, etc.)
- Advanced blast and CBR modeling of building and systems (structural damage, interior and exterior plume dispersion, safe haven areas)
- Advanced evacuation planning and routing to include test of mass notification system, training, and exercises
- Advanced disaster response and recovery planning in conjunction with neighbors and local government

Data Gap Analysis. The Assessment Team may feel that the data gathered for on-site assessment are not enough. The Team should assess the following information:

- Do we know where the greatest damages may occur in the threat/ hazard areas?
- Do we know whether critical facilities will be operational after a threat/hazard event?
- Are there enough data to determine which assets are subject to the greatest potential damages?
- Are there enough data to determine whether significant elements of the community are vulnerable to potential threats?
- Are there enough data to determine whether certain areas of historic, environmental, political, or cultural significance are vulnerable to potential threats?
- Is there concern about a particular threat because of its severity, frequency, or likelihood of occurrence?
- Are additional data needed to justify the expenditure of community or state funds for mitigation initiatives?

If the Team decides that more data will be beneficial to conduct the assessment, a determination should be made as to what type of data are needed and what resources are available for collecting new data. If stakeholders and the Team agree on collecting new data, the Team needs to prioritize areas for additional data collection.

Vulnerability Assessment Methodologies

There are a number of methods for conducting a vulnerability assessment and some examples are given next. Seek advice on deciding which is the best vulnerability assessment methodology for you. It may be that some funding sources require that a particular methodology is used. It could be that one methodology is more appropriate for your particular circumstances. For instance, if you are in charge of a facility that is an administrative building, you could choose to use a methodology that is people based.

The following is a brief overview of some vulnerability assessment methodologies.

Classification Assessment

A classification assessment is based on the size of the facility, the number of people employed there and the nature of work carried out. For instance, a small branch office employing 10 people, one that has little volume public contact or a typical store front type operation would get a low vulnerability rating.

Remember

A larger facility, one that employs up to 150 people, one that has moderate volume public contact would get a medium low rating. A facility that employs up to 450 people, one that has moderate to high volume public contact and one that performs a government or administrative function such as a court house, tax office, regional, state or government office, manufacturing or health care facility, would get a medium high rating. A high vulnerability rating would go to facilities with more than 450 employees, a multi-story building, high volume public contact, high risk function such as local schools, law enforcement offices, district courts, regional FBI offices, manufacturing facility and so on.

Building Inherent Vulnerability Assessment

A building inherent vulnerability assessment is based on:
- ☐ Asset visibility - do people know what you do
- ☐ Target Utility – Are you a low, medium or high risk target
- ☐ Asset Accessibility – is your location remote and secure or is it in an urban setting with open access and unrestricted parking
- ☐ Asset Mobility – Are assets moved regularly or fixed
- ☐ Hazardous Materials – are there no hazardous materials or are large quantities stored onsite
- ☐ Collateral Damage Potential – is there no risk or could the collateral damage extend out a mile or more
- ☐ Site Population/Capacity – how many people are involved from none to thousands.

Remember

Each of these categories is given a rating (0 to 5) or low, medium or high, and the collective rating is your facility vulnerability assessment rating.

The DOJ, Office of Justice Programs (OJP) provides an objective approach to determining vulnerability (U.S. Department of Justice, State Domestic Preparedness Equipment Program, Assessment and Strategy Development Tool Kit). It requires the rating of the following areas:

1. Level of Visibility

What is the perceived awareness of the target's existence and the visibility of the target to the general populace, or to the terrorist in particular?

2. Asset Value of Target Site (Individual Asset or Assets Accumulated within the building)

What is the usefulness of the asset(s) to the population, economy, government, company, or organization? Also consider the impact on continuity of operations, hampering of emergency response, and general potential consequences. This could be used more than once if the value of the asset(s) impacts more than one critical area.

3. Target Value to Potential Threat Element/Aggressor

Does the target serve the ends of the aggressors Assessment based on motivations (political, religious, racial, environmental, and special interests)?

4. Aggressor Access to Target

Does the target have available ingress and egress for a potential aggressor?

5. Target Threat of Hazard

Are CBR materials present in quantities that could become hazardous if released? These quantities could be on site or in relatively close proximity so that a theft or an accident could render them a hazard to the building or site. Take into consideration distance from building (a 1-mile radius is suggested around the building), the prevailing wind direction, the slope of the terrain, and the quantity of materials present.

6. Site Population Capacity

What is the maximum number of individuals at the building or site at a given time? This could be standard worst case occupancy during an average day or peak occupancy at a designated time (e.g., a movie theater).

7. Potential for Collateral Damage (Mass Casualties)

Address potential collateral mass casualties within a 1-mile radius of the target site. Number ranges indicate inhabitants within a 1-mile radius of the site.

Each of your facilities can then be assessed and scored. The total building score provides an analysis of building vulnerability from a site perspective. This methodology can be applied to all building types. The result is independent of facility/occupancy type, except for the type of influence on population and siting.

Professionals in the private sector and at all levels of government are unanimous in their opinions that it is not a question of if another devastating terrorist event will occur, but when and where it will occur. In an ongoing study, the Rutgers Center for the Study of Public Security is conducting a survey to discover how law enforcement officials in the United States assess their local terrorist threat. Eighty percent of the almost 1,400 respondents who were surveyed expect a terrorist event to occur in their jurisdiction —most likely a cyberterrorism or conventional attack. Almost all respondents reported that at least one terrorist group is present in their jurisdiction.

An alternate approach (see below) uses a simplified matrix to rank the order of buildings using a numerical score of 1 (low) to 5 (high). The evaluation factors can be developed for each building use or owner-specific criteria. The factors shown illustrate a health care provider scenario:

☐ Criticality of Function: How critical is the building and function to the organization?

☐ Location: Is the building near federal buildings, major transportation, or iconic properties?

☐ Occupancy of Building: Are occupants mobile or non-ambulatory?

☐ Involvement in Community: Does the building or staff provide unique capabilities?

☐ Critical External Commitments: Does the building support other organizations or missions?

Building	Criticality of Function	Location	Occupancy of Building	Involvement in Community	Critical External Commitments	Total Score
Headquarters	2	5	3	1	4	15
Hospital 1	1	2	2	1	1	7
Hospital 2	3	2	3	4	4	16
Data Center	5	4	3	3	2	17

Source: FEMA

The objective is to provide an analysis of a building, facility, or site and to identify the buildings that are most vulnerable from a given threat/hazard matched against specific building type or function. Having the ranked list of buildings, the next step is to conduct an in-depth vulnerability assessment of the building. The building assessment is to evaluate specific design and architectural features and identify all vulnerabilities of the building functions and building systems. Frequently, single-point-vulnerabilities exist, which are critical functions or systems that lack redundancy and, if damaged by an attack, would result in immediate organization disruption or loss of capability. These are generally the highest risk vulnerabilities.

Remember

Risk Assessment

The risk assessment uses the threat, asset value and vulnerability assessments to determine the level of risk for each critical asset against each applicable threat. This takes into account the likelihood of the threat occurring (probability) and the effects (consequences) of the occurrence if the critical asset is damaged or destroyed.

Remember The risk assessment provides security consultants, engineers, designers and architects with a relative risk profile that defines which assets are at the greatest risk against specific threats.

Any threat subjects an organization to risk. Therefore, when a threat is exhibited, a risk rating needs to be applied in order to understand how to manage the risk. A threat management team should have processes and procedures in place for measuring the probability of loss and the severity of loss, in light of a threat.

The following primary risk types should be considered in determining risk exposure:

☐ Mission or function risks

☐ Asset risks; and

☐ Security risks.

There are a number of risk assessment methodologies and some rely on complex formulas to determine each risk threat.

Our methodology is simpler and depends on identifying and prioritizing all critical assets, threats and vulnerabilities which you should have done by now. You then have to decide what risk each critical asset faces. Is there a low, medium or high risk of that asset being attacked, damaged, or destroyed? This analysis gives you your threat rating and will determine your priorities when it comes to mitigation in Step Three – Gap Closure. Risk analysis not only determines risk exposure, it allows organizations to integrate financial objectives with security objectives.

The Department of Homeland Security's Office of Domestic Preparedness states that the important steps to performing a risk analysis are:

* Identify risks
* Determine impact of threats and
* Balance impact of threats with safeguards

Worksheet: Site Functional Pre-Assessment Matrix

	Low Risk	Medium Risk	High Risk
Risk Factors Total	1-60	61-175	≥ 176

Function	Cyber Attack	Vehicle Bomb	Suicide Bomber	Chemical (Sarin)	Biological (Ricin)
Administration					
Asset Value					
Threat Rating					
Vulnerability Rating					
Engineering					
Asset Value					
Threat Rating					
Vulnerability Rating					
Warehousing					
Asset Value					
Threat Rating					
Vulnerability Rating					
Data Center					
Asset Value					
Threat Rating					
Vulnerability Rating					
Food Service					
Asset Value					
Threat Rating					
Vulnerability Rating					
Security					
Asset Value					
Threat Rating					
Vulnerability Rating					
Housekeeping					
Asset Value					
Threat Rating					
Vulnerability Rating					
Day Care					
Asset Value					
Threat Rating					
Vulnerability Rating					

Source: FEMA

Worksheet Site Infrastructure Systems Pre-Assessment Matrix

Infrastructure	Cyber Attack	Vehicle Bomb	Suicide Bomber	Chemical (Sarin)	Biological (Ricin)
Site					
Asset Value					
Threat Rating					
Vulnerability Rating					
Architectural					
Asset Value					
Threat Rating					
Vulnerability Rating					
Structural Systems					
Asset Value					
Threat Rating					
Vulnerability Rating					
Envelope Systems					
Asset Value					
Threat Rating					
Vulnerability Rating					
Utility Systems					
Asset Value					
Threat Rating					
Vulnerability Rating					
Mechanical Systems					
Asset Value					
Threat Rating					
Vulnerability Rating					
Plumbing and Gas Systems					
Asset Value					
Threat Rating					
Vulnerability Rating					
Electrical Systems					
Asset Value					
Threat Rating					
Vulnerability Rating					
Fire Alarm Systems					
Asset Value					
Threat Rating					
Vulnerability Rating					
IT/Communications Systems					
Asset Value					
Threat Rating					
Vulnerability Rating					

Source: FEMA

Prioritization of observations

Once you have identified your risks you can give each one a risk rating. When vulnerabilities are high and the threat is evident, the risk of exploitation is greater.

Remember

As a result, a higher priority for asset protection should be considered. When the vulnerability is low and the terrorist has little capability to exploit the vulnerability, now or in the future, the risk is less and the priority for new countermeasures for this asset will be lower. The areas of greatest risk will become the basis for deciding where to focus additional countermeasures and what kind of countermeasures to apply.

The acceptable level of risk will not be determined by a formula. Risk levels will vary with time, circumstances, and management attitude toward risk in the organization decide what constitutes an acceptable level of risk. Judgments made regarding impact, threat, and vulnerability will help determine risk priorities.

Risk Evaluation

Ten Risk Methodology Evaluation Criteria

Checklist

☐ Clearly Identify the Infrastructure Sector Being Assessed

☐ Specify the Type of Security Discipline Addressed, e.g. Physical, Information, Operations

☐ Collect Specific Data Pertaining to Each Asset

☐ Identify Critical/Key Assets to be Protected

☐ Determine the Mission Impact of the Loss or Damage of that Asset

☐ Conduct a Threat Analysis and Perform Assessment for Specific Assets

☐ Perform a Vulnerability Analysis and Assessment to Specific Threats

☐ Conduct Analytical Risk Assessment and Determine Priorities for each Asset

☐ Be Relatively Low Cost to Train and Conduct

☐ Make Specific, Concrete Recommendations Concerning Countermeasures

Risk Management

Traditionally, the building regulatory system has addressed natural disaster mitigation (fire, hurricane, tornado, flood, earthquake, windstorm, and snow storm) through prescriptive building codes supported by well-established and accepted reference standards, regulations, inspection, and assessment techniques. Some man-made risks (e.g., HazMat storage) and specific societal goals (energy conservation and life safety) have also been similarly addressed. However, the building regulation system has not yet fully addressed most manmade hazards or terrorist threats.

Soon after September 11, 2001, the New York City Building Department initiated an effort to analyze the building code with regard to terrorist threats. The task force issued a report recommending code changes based on the attack on the World Trade Center. The National Fire Protection Association (NFPA) has a committee on premises security and security system installation standards. These advances may some day result in the building regulatory system developing more prescriptive building codes to mitigate security threats.

For most cases across the United States, the threats and risks for a specific building will be low. For buildings at a higher threat and risk, higher standards and performance may be required. In every design and renovation project, the owner ultimately has three choices when addressing the risk posed by terrorism. He or she can:

☐ Do nothing and accept the risk

☐ Perform a risk assessment and manage the risk by installing reasonable mitigation measures

☐ Harden the building against all threats to achieve the least amount of risk

---

Countermeasures are actions, devices, or systems employed to eliminate, reduce, or mitigate risk and vulnerability. To assist in making studied decisions that can be supported over time, multiple countermeasure packages that recommend appropriate actions should be provided. Options are often characterized as follows:

- Risk averse package: The preferred option, unconstrained by financial or political considerations. This package provides a point of reference for the expenditure necessary to minimize risk most effectively. This option is designed to reduce risk to the greatest degree possible.

- Risk tolerant package: The option that strikes a balance between the needs of security and protection and the financial and political constraints of a state or municipality.

- Risk acceptance package: The least desired option, which typically reflects the highest acceptable amount of risk, but represents the least possible cost.

Countermeasures, such as expansion of staffing, installation of equipment and new technology, or target hardening, must be evaluated or tested periodically to ensure that improvements are actually working as intended. These evaluations and tests should verify that policies and procedures are in place to guide how the countermeasures will be used. Countermeasures include physical security (fencing, camera surveillance, seismic monitoring devices, and barricades), cyber security (firewalls, antivirus software, secure computer networks), personnel security, and other proactive methods that industry uses to secure critical infrastructure.

Risk Management Choices Chart

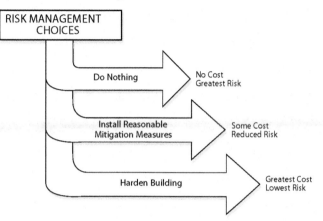

Summary

If you have followed all the steps in this Gap Analysis chapter you should now have determined the key roles of your facility, the critical assets that need to be protected, the threats they face, how vulnerable they are and the actual risk they pose.

Armed with this knowledge you are now able to proceed to the next chapter – Step Three: Gap Closure - which reviews the security options available to you.

STEP THREE: GAP CLOSURE

Introduction

 Must Do

Having identified your risks it is time to mitigate them. You have to look at your current security situation and determine what needs to be done to most effectively close the identified gaps – to mitigate against each identified vulnerability. Use the Assessment Checklist to work through all key areas and for every identified threat and vulnerability come up with the most appropriate mitigating option. This is your Gap Closure.

Because it is not possible to completely eliminate risk, and every project has resource limitations, you must analyze how mitigation measures would affect risk and decide on the best and most cost-effective measures to implement to achieve the desired level of protection (risk management).

The first goal of an integrated physical protection system is protection of the facility and all its assets. The second goal is to deter would be aggressors. Ideally, you achieve this by making the facility and its approaches so secure and so difficult to penetrate that they look for an easier target. However, a determined aggressor, especially a terrorist, may not be deterred so easily so the third goal is to do everything possible to detect any intruders as early as possible, then delay them long enough so that they can be intercepted before they reach their target.

 Remember

When considering your options remember that the goal is to close the security gaps – to put in place procedures and systems that protect your critical assets and eliminate weak spots and vulnerabilities.

All the options available to you can be categorized under the headings of prevention, deterrence, detection, delay and response and all will be dealt with in this chapter and in much greater detail in the technical section in part two of this manual.

It is important to remember that a facility may contain several different security layers with different access portals and control points. Integrating these layers and their varying degrees of security into the physical protection system can pose serious challenges and needs careful planning so that the appropriate level of security is maintained with minimal disruption to day to day operating procedures.

You must also recognize the difference approaches that need to be taken depending on the age of your facility. If you are constructing a new building you can incorporate the latest and greatest – budget permitting - in order to meet your security needs. If you are installing a physical protection system in an old building you may have to overcome a number of building and construction challenges and if you are updating a previously installed security system, you will have to consider carefully what can be retained and what new devices will be needed.

Key Points

* Gap Closure – Vulnerability Mitigation

* Gaps per risk level (highest to lowest)

* Identify mitigation concept to lower risk for each vulnerability

* Identify measures (Physical Protection/Cyber and/or Ops or Procedural)

* Re evaluate risks, Scenario based assessment (are gaps closed?)

* Identify coordination/ integration w/ other systems required

* ROM cost per mitigation - Unit cost X no of units

Understanding Security Layers

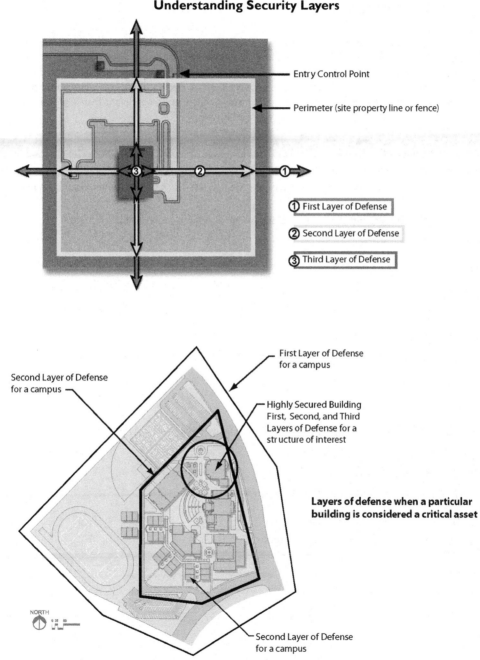

Entry Control Point

Perimeter (site property line or fence)

① First Layer of Defense

② Second Layer of Defense

③ Third Layer of Defense

First Layer of Defense
for a campus

Second Layer of Defense
for a campus

Highly Secured Building
First, Second, and Third
Layers of Defense for a
structure of interest

**Layers of defense when a particular
building is considered a critical asset**

Second Layer of Defense
for a campus

NORTH

The Elements of an Integrated Physical Security System

Remember

The most important part of any integrated physical security system is integration. A system has to be fully integrated and incorporate all interdependencies if it is to be successful. The basic elements of an IPS system are deterrence, detection and delay and you have to ask yourself which of these is the most important. Is the most critical thing to a) deter, b) detect or c) delay? If you answered a, b or c you are wrong. An integrated physical security system means that everything is integrated and no one part is more important than any other. They all have to work together if the IPS system is going to work effectively.

Deter	Detection	Delay	Response
Discourage access	Intrusion sensing	Barriers	Interruption
	Alarm Communication	Dispensable barriers	Communication to response force
	Entry Control	Deployment of response force	Neutralization

Deter

☐ Barriers, sensors, fences, access controls

☐ Signage

☐ Visible cameras

☐ Guard stations

☐ Dogs

☐ Patrols

Detection

☐ Sensor Activated - Alarm Signal Initiated - Alarm Reported - Alarm Assessed

Performance Measures

☐ Probability of detection

☐ Time for communication and assessment

☐ Frequency of nuisance alarms

☐ Alarm without assessment is not detection

Elements of Access Delay

Protective Force Guards

Flexible
Continuous Operational Cost
Sensitive to Numbers
Subject to Compromise

Barriers

In Place; Fail Secure
Commercially Available
Weak Against Explosives
Operational; Aesthetic Limits

Dispensable Barriers

Compact; Rapidly Deployed
Maximize Delay at Target
"Somewhat" Threat Independent
Spurious Activation; Safety Concerns

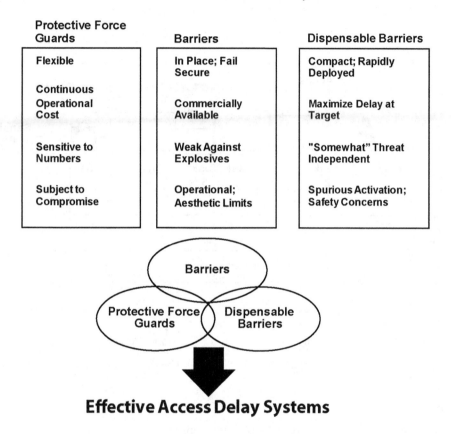

Effective Access Delay Systems

Adversary Theft Path

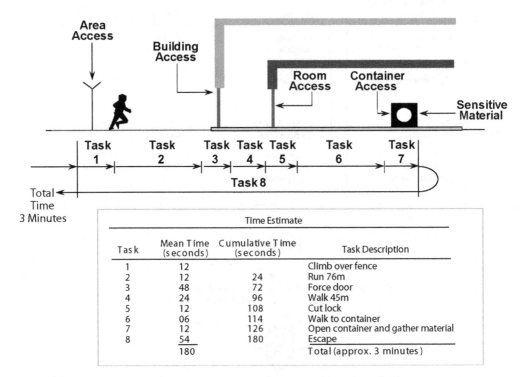

Task	Mean Time (seconds)	Cumulative Time (seconds)	Task Description
		Time Estimate	
1	12		Climb over fence
2	12	24	Run 76m
3	48	72	Force door
4	24	96	Walk 45m
5	12	108	Cut lock
6	06	114	Walk to container
7	12	126	Open container and gather material
8	54	180	Escape
	180		Total (approx. 3 minutes)

Response

☐ Communicate to response force - Deploy Response Force - Neutralize adversary

Performance measures:

☐ Probability of communication to response force

☐ Time to communicate

☐ Probability of deployment to adversary location

☐ Time to deploy

☐ Response force effectiveness

Remember

Summary: Response time is critical. The goal is to have systems in place that a) deter would be adversaries , and b) if they do attack the facility, to have adequate measures that detect them and slow them down long enough so that you can initiate the appropriate response and intercept them before they reach their objective. The quicker the attackers can be intercepted and neutralized the less damage they can cause.

Security Principles

The components of security include deception, intelligence, operational protection, and structural hardening. Ideally, a potential terrorist attack is prevented or pre-empted through intelligence measures. If the attack does occur, physical security measures combine with operational forces (e.g., surveillance, guards, and sensors) to provide layers of defense that delay and/or thwart the attack. Deception may be used to make the facility appear to be a more protected or lower-risk facility than it actually is, thereby making it appear to be a less attractive target. Deception can also be used to misdirect the attacker to a portion of the facility that is non-critical. As a last resort, structural hardening is provided to save lives and facilitate evacuation and rescue by preventing building collapse and limiting flying debris.

Because of the interrelationship between physical and operational security measures, it is imperative for the owner and security professional to define early in the design process what extent of operational security is planned for various threat levels.

An effective way to implement these goals is to create layers of security within the facility. The outermost layer is the perimeter of the facility. Interior to this line is the approach zone to the facility, then the building exterior, and finally the building interior. The interior of the building may be divided into successively more protected zones, starting with publicly accessible areas such as the lobby and retail space, to the more private areas of offices, and finally the vital functions such as the control room and emergency functions. The advantage of this approach is that once a line of protection is breached, the facility has not been completely compromised. Having multiple lines of defense provides redundancy to the security system, adding robustness to the design. Also, by using this approach, not all of the focus is on the outer layer of protection, which may lead to an unattractive, fortress-like appearance.

Tips

To provide a reliable design, each ring must have a uniform level of security provided along its entire length; security is only as strong as the weakest link.

To have a balanced design, both physical and operational security measures need to be implemented in the facility. Architects and engineers can contribute to an effective physical security system, which augments and facilitates the operational security functions. If security measures are left as an afterthought, expensive, unattractive, and make-shift security posts are the inevitable result.

This is a good time to revisit Crime Prevention Through Environmental Design (CPTED). The three basic elements of CPTED are natural access controls, natural surveillance and territorial reinforcement. Natural access controls include landscaping, fencing and so on to control entry to a neighborhood or area. Natural surveillance in design terms means giving people maximum visibility in order to see and be seen in the spaces around them. Territorial reinforcement uses buildings and other structures in order to establish "ownership" i.e. it enables people to determine who belongs there and who doesn't. There are great lessons to be learned from CPTED and applying its elements and techniques is a good way of designing out potential security threats.

The Integrated Physical Security Handbook

Scenario V Mitigation Worksheet #5 Sample

SCENARIO V MITIGATION WORKSHEET #5 SAMPLE

Example

Vulnerability	Gap Closure/ Mitigation Concept	Mitigation Catagory			
		Detect	Delay	Assess	Respond
One card access system - allows access to all employees to all rooms on campus 24/7. There is no way to detect entry to critical areas on site	Replace or upgrade to a programmable card access system, allowing authorized & monitored access only to each area	X		X	
Passwords are not personal & not protected,	Develop a protocol / policy for protecting and issuing personal passwords		X		
Lack of redundancy / no backup systems	Engineer redundant systems and /or contacts with other facilities that can provide temporary services if sytems are disrupted		X		
Employee not flagged as a threat	Implement better communications with employees, involve HR	X			
To date there has been no training to respond to breach of access contol at this facility	Contract with external security contractor to respond to a breach in access control				X

Objective:

To identify appropriate Gap closure solutions to all areas of vulnerability.

Master Mitigation Worksheet #6 Sample

MASTER MITIGATION WORKSHEET #6 SAMPLE

Objective:	Develop an Intergrated Master Mitigation Chart
Book Step :	Step # 3 - Gap Closure
Purpose:	The 2nd phase in the gap closure process is to develop" Catch All" Mitigation list
	This list will integrate all of the scenario based mitigation concepts into one table, and provide a ROM cost estimate for your future security upgrades in a phased execution schedule.
Note:	This chart will allow you to develop your security strategic plan stratagy based on cost and " Best bang for your Buck"

Action1.	A - List Gap closure concepts & systems from previous WS #5 Column B
Action 2.	B - Identify if this is a new system or an upgrade to a current existing system
Action 3.	C - Develop a Rough Order of Magnitude (ROM) cost estimate for each gap closure concept. This cost must be a total of: 1st cost, recurring cost , operational costs.
Action 4.	D - Identify if this is a priority 1, 2, 3 activity
	1 - Must do in the short term (immediately)
	2 - next year
	3 - 2 to 5 years out (long term)

Example

A	B	C				D
Gap Closure / Mitigation Concept	New or Tie-in to existing system	ROM $ Estimate				Phasing
		1st Cost	Recuring	Ops. Cost	Total Cost	
Replace or upgrade to a programmable card access system, allowing authorized & monitored access only to each area	Upgrade existing system	$12,000	$500	$300 per year	$13,000	2

Objective:

To develop an integrated master mitigation chart

See end of this chapter for examples of completed worksheets and see end of the book for blank worksheets that you can use.

External Options

Perimeter Protection

Perimeter protection is extremely important for urban buildings because in most cases, the facility perimeter is defined by the external walls of the building. There is no buffer zone with wires, fences and controlled access points to keep terrorists and others a safe distance away from your building.

Must Do

The perimeter line of protection is the outermost line that can be protected by facility security measures. The perimeter needs to be designed to prevent incursions or carriers of large-scale weapons from gaining access to the site. In design, it is assumed that all large-scale explosive weapons (i.e. car bombs or truck bombs) are outside this line of defense. This line is defended by both physical and operational security methods.

Many times, vulnerable buildings are located in urban areas where site conditions are tight. In this case, the options are obviously limited. Often, the perimeter line can be pushed out to the edge of the sidewalk by means of bollards, planters, and other obstacles. To push this line even further outward, restricting or eliminating parking along the curb can be arranged with the local authorities, but this can be a difficult and time consuming effort. In some cases, eliminating loading zones and street/lane closings are an option.

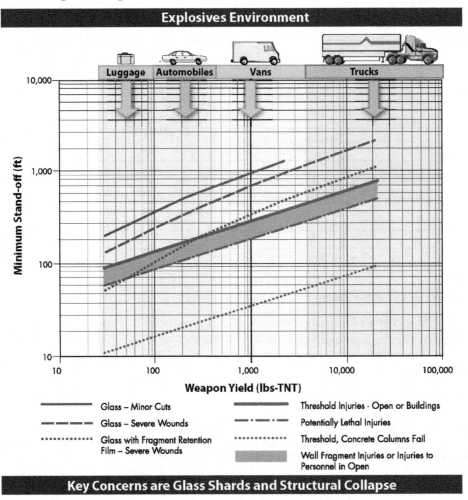

Explosive environments - blast range to effect

Stand Off Distance

The distance between an asset and a threat is referred to as the stand-off distance. There is no ideal stand-off distance but the greater the distance between the asset and the threat the less the damage that is likely to be caused. Obviously the damage will depend on the size of the explosion, the construction of the building and the level of protection but the most cost-effective solution for mitigating explosive effects is to ensure the explosions occur as far away from the buildings as possible. A major consideration is, of course, whether you are in an urban or rural setting because that is likely to determine how far your perimeter line is from your building.

Considerations for stand-off distance are as follows:

The first mode of site protection is to create "keep out zones" that can ensure a minimum guaranteed distance between an explosion (e.g., from a vehicle) and the target structure.

The perimeter line is the outermost line that can be protected by the security measures incorporated during the design process. It is recommended that the perimeter line be located as far as is practical from the building exterior. Many vulnerable buildings are located in urban areas where only the exterior wall of the building stands between the outside world and the building occupants. In this case, the options are obviously limited. Often, the perimeter line can be pushed out to the edge of the sidewalk by means of bollards, planters, and other obstacles. To push this line even further outward, restricting or eliminating parking along the curb often can be coordinated with local authorities. In some extreme cases, elimination of loading zones and the closure of streets are an option.

Tips

"Keep out zones" can be achieved with perimeter barriers that cannot be compromised by vehicular ramming. A continuous line of security should be installed along the perimeter of the site to protect it from unscreened vehicles and to keep all vehicles as far away from critical assets as possible.

When selecting a site for a new building, consider its location relative to the site perimeter. Maximize the distance between the perimeter fence and developed areas, providing as much open space as possible inside the fence along the site perimeter.

The following critical building components should be located away from main entrances, vehicle circulation, parking, and maintenance areas. If this is not possible, harden as appropriate:

- ☐ Emergency generator, including fuel systems, day tank, fire sprinkler, and water supply
- ☐ Normal fuel storage
- ☐ Telephone distribution and main switchgear
- ☐ Fire pumps
- ☐ Building control centers
- ☐ UPS systems powering critical functions

☐ Main refrigeration systems if critical to building operation

☐ Elevator machinery and controls

☐ Shafts for stairs, elevators, and utilities

☐ Critical distribution feeders for emergency power

Note: As with mitigating efforts, there is no reason why your preferred solutions should not only be effective but also aesthetically pleasing.

Controlled Access Zones

Access control refers to points of controlled access to the facility through the perimeter line. The controlled access check or inspection points for vehicles require architectural features or barriers to maintain the defensible perimeter. Architects and engineers can accommodate these security functions by providing adequate design for these areas, which makes it difficult for a vehicle to crash onto the site. Remember that you may have to implement different security layers at different points around or close to the perimeter and these will have to be planned into your physical protection system.

Deterrence and delay are major attributes of the perimeter security design that should be consistent with the landscaping objectives, such as emphasizing the open nature characterizing high-population buildings.

Remember

Since it is impossible to thwart all possible threats, the objective is to make it difficult to successfully execute the easiest attack scenarios such as a car bomb detonated along the curb, or a vehicle jumping the curb and ramming into the building prior to detonation.

If space is available between the perimeter line and the building exterior, much can be done to delay an intruder. Examples include terraced landscaping, fountains, statues, staircases, circular driveways, planters, trees, high-strength cables hidden in bushes and any number of other obstacles that make it difficult to rapidly reach the building. Though individually these features may not be able to stop a vehicle, in combination, they form a daunting obstacle course. Other ideas for implementing secure landscaping features may be found in texts on Crime.

Prevention Through Environmental Design (CPTED). These concepts are useful for slowing down traffic, improving surveillance, and site circulation. On the sides of the building that are close to the curb, where landscaping solutions are limited, anti-ram barriers capable of stopping a vehicle on impact are recommended for high-risk buildings. Barrier design methods are discussed in more detail below. The location of access points should be oblique to oncoming streets so that it is difficult for a vehicle to gain enough velocity to break through these access locations. If the site provides straight-on access to the building, some mitigation options include concrete medians in the street to slow vehicles or, for high-risk buildings, use of anti-ram barriers along the curb capable of withstanding the impact of high-velocity vehicles.

Place parking as far as practical from the building. Off-site parking is recommended for high-risk facilities vulnerable to terrorist attack. If onsite surface parking or underground parking is provided, take precautions such as limiting access to these areas only to the building occupants and/or having all vehicles inspected in areas close-in to the building. If an underground area is used for a high-risk building, the garage should be placed adjacent to the building under a plaza area rather than directly underneath the building. To the extent practical, limit the size of vehicle that is able to enter the garage by imposing physical barriers on vehicle height.

Must Do

Clear zones should be maintained on both sides of the perimeter barrier to provide an unobstructed view of the barrier and the ground adjacent to it. A clear zone of 20 feet or more should exist between the perimeter barrier and exterior structures, parking areas, and natural or manmade features. When possible, a clear zone of 50 feet or more should exist between the perimeter barrier and structures within the protected area, except when the wall of a building constitutes part of the perimeter barrier. Roads within the clear zone should be as close to the perimeter barrier as possible without interfering with it. The roads should be constructed to allow effective road barriers to deter motor movement of unauthorized personnel. When barriers enclose a large area, a perimeter road should be provided for security patrol vehicles on the interior.

Fences may be augmented with additional security systems, such as motion sensors and close circuit camera systems.

Because barriers can be compromised through breaching (cutting a hole through a fence) or by nature (berms eroded by the wind and rain), they should be inspected and maintained at least weekly. Security personnel should look for signs of deliberate breaches, holes in and under barriers, natural debris building up against barriers, and the proper functioning of locks.

Approaches and Speed Control

Most roads tend to be straight because this allows traffic to move more quickly than constant twists and turns. It also allows terrorists to accelerate as they approach your building.

A bollard can stop a 15,000-pound truck moving at 35 miles per hour but may not be able to stop the same truck moving at 55 miles per hour. Anything that forces the truck to slow down as it approaches your building will increase the effectiveness of perimeter protection barriers whether they are high curbs, bollards, berms or even strategically planted trees.

Wherever possible the vehicle approach should be parallel to the building. Another technique is to construct a serpentine (curving) approach with tight-radius corners. Existing streets can be retrofitted with barriers, bollards, swing gates, or other measures to force vehicles to travel in a serpentine path. Again, high curbs and other measures should be installed to keep vehicles from departing the roadway in an effort to avoid these countermeasures.

> **Remember**
>
> Less radical traffic calming strategies can also be implemented. These include raised crosswalks, speed humps and speed tables, pavement treatments and traffic circles. Speed humps and speed tables can both be used to control a vehicle's speed. These should not be confused with speed bumps which should only be used in low speed areas such as parking lots.

Physical Protective Barriers

Protective barriers are used to define the physical limits of an installation, activity, or area. Barriers restrict, channel, or impede access and are fully integrated to form a continuous obstacle around the building or facility. They are designed to deter the worst-case threat. The barriers should be focused on providing assets with an acceptable level of protection against a threat.

Protective barriers form the perimeter of controlled, limited, and exclusion areas. Utility areas (such as water sources, transformer banks, commercial power and fuel connections, heating and power plants, or air conditioning units) may require these barriers for safety standards.

Protective barriers consist of two major categories—natural and structural.

☐ Natural protective barriers are mountains and deserts, cliffs and ditches, water obstacles, or other terrain features that are difficult to traverse.

☐ Structural protective barriers are man-made devices (such as fences, walls, floors, roofs, grills, bars, roadblocks, signs, or other construction) used to restrict, channel, or impede access.

Barriers offer important benefits to a physical-security posture. They create a psychological deterrent for anyone thinking of unauthorized entry.

They may delay or even prevent passage through them. This is especially true of barriers against forced entry and vehicles. Barriers have a direct impact on the number of security posts needed and on the frequency of use for each post.

Barriers cannot be designed for all situations. Considerations for protective structural barriers include the following:

☐ Weighing the cost of completely enclosing large tracts of land with significant structural barriers against the threat and the cost of alternate security precautions (such as patrols, MWD teams, ground sensors, electronic surveillance, and airborne sensors).

☐ Sizing a restricted area based on the degree of compartmentalization required and the area's complexity. As a rule, size should be kept to a minimum consistent with operational efficiency. A restricted area's size may be driven by the likelihood of an aggressor's use of certain tactics.

For example, protecting assets from a vehicle bomb often calls for a substantial explosives standoff distance. In these cases, mitigating the vehicle bomb would often be more important than minimizing the restricted area to the extent necessary for operational efficiency.

Protective barriers should be established for—

☐ Controlling vehicular and pedestrian traffic flow

☐ Providing entry-control points where ID can be checked

☐ Defining a buffer zone for more highly classified areas

☐ Precluding visual compromise by unauthorized individuals

☐ Delaying forced entry

☐ Protecting individual assets.

If a secured area requires a limited or exclusion area on a temporary or infrequent basis, it may not be possible to use physical structural barriers. A temporary limited or exclusion area may be established where the lack of proper physical barriers is compensated for by additional security posts, patrols, and other security measures during the period of restriction.

Tips

There are two basic categories of perimeter anti-ram barriers; passive (or fixed) and active (or operable). Each is described below.

Passive Systems

Passive barriers are those that are fixed in place and do not allow for vehicle entry. These are to be used away from vehicle access points. The majority of these are constructed in place.

For lower-risk buildings without straight-on vehicular access, it may be appropriate to install surface-mounted systems such as planters, or to use landscaping features to deter an intrusion threat. An example of a simple but effective landscaping solution is to install a deep permanent planter around the building with a wall that is as high as a car or truck bumper.

Individual planters mounted on the sidewalk resist impact through inertia and friction between the planter and the pavement. It can be expected that the planter will move as a result of the impact. For a successful design, the maximum displacement of the planter should be less than the setback distance to the building. The structure supporting the weight of the planter must be considered prior to installation.

Tips

To further reduce displacement, the planter may be placed several inches below the pavement surface. A roughened, grouted interface surface will also improve performance. The traditional anti-ram solution entails the use of bollards. Bollards are concrete-filled steel pipes that are placed every few feet along the curb of a sidewalk to prevent vehicle intrusion. In order for them to resist the impact of a vehicle, the bollard needs to be fully embedded into a concrete strip foundation that is several feet deep. The height of the bollard above ground should be higher than the bumper of the vehicle. The spacing of the bollards is based on several factors including ADA (American Disabilities Act) requirements, the minimum width of a vehicle, and the number of bollards required to resist the impact. As a rule of thumb, the center-to-center spacing should be between three and five feet to be effective. The height of the bollard is to be at least as high as the bumper of the design threat vehicle, which is taken typically between two and three feet. An alternative to a bollard is a plinth wall, which is a continuous knee wall constructed of reinforced concrete with a buried foundation. The wall may be fashioned into a bench, a base for a fence, or the wall of a planter. To be effective, the height needs to be at least as high as the vehicle bumper.

For effectiveness, the barriers need to be placed as close to the curb as possible. However, the property line of buildings often does not extend to the curb. Therefore, to place barriers with foundations near the curb, a permit is required by the local authorities, which can be a difficult time-consuming effort to obtain. To avoid this, building owners are often inclined to place bollards along the property line, which significantly reduces the effectiveness of the barrier system.

The foundation of the bollard and plinth wall system can present challenges. There are sometimes vaults or basements below the pavement that extend to the property line, which often require special foundation details. Unless the foundation wall can sustain the reaction forces, significant damage may occur.

Tips

Below-ground utilities that are frequently close to the pavement surface present additional problems. Their location may not be known with certainty, and this often leads to difficulties during construction. This also can be a strong deterrent to selecting barriers with foundations as a solution. However, for high-risk facilities, it is recommended that these issues be resolved during the design phase so that a reliable anti-ram barrier solution can be installed. For lower-risk buildings without straight-on vehicular access, it may be more appropriate to install surface-mounted systems such as planters or to use landscaping features to deter an intrusion threat. An example of a simple but effective landscaping solution is to install a deep permanent planter around the building with a wall that is at least as high as a car or truck bumper.

Active Systems

At vehicular access points, active or operational anti-ram systems are required. There are off-the-shelf products available that have been rated to resist various levels of car and truck impacts. Solutions include:

- ☐ crash gates;
- ☐ surface-mounted plate systems;

☐ retractable bollards; and

☐ rotating-wedge systems.

The first three systems listed generally have lower impact ratings than the last two listed. Check with the manufacturer to ensure that the system has been tested to meet the impact requirements for your project.

It is important that the installation of hydraulically operated systems be performed by a qualified contractor to ensure a reliable system that will work properly in all weather conditions.

Effectiveness of Anti-Ram Barriers

The effectiveness of an anti-ram barrier is based on the amount of energy it can absorb versus the amount of kinetic energy imparted by vehicle impact. The angle of approach reduces this energy in non-head on situations, and the energy absorbed by the crushing of the vehicle also reduces the energy imparted to the barriers. The kinetic energy imparted to the wall is one-half the product of the vehicle mass and its impact velocity squared. Because the velocity term is squared, a change in velocity affects the energy level more than a change in vehicle weight.

For this reason, it is important to review lines of approach to define areas where a vehicle has a long, straight road to pick up speed before impact.

The vehicle weight used for the design of barriers typically ranges from 4000 lb for cars up to 15,000 lb for trucks. Impact velocities typically range from 30 mph for oblique impact areas (i.e., where the oncoming street is parallel to the curb) up to 50 mph where there is straight-on access (i.e., where the oncoming street is perpendicular to the curb).

The kinetic energy of the vehicle at impact is absorbed by the barrier system. For fixed systems (like a concrete bollard), the energy is absorbed through the deformational strain energy absorbed by the barrier, soil, and the vehicle. For movable systems (like a surface-mounted planter) energy is absorbed through shear friction against the pavement and vehicle deformation.

Barrier effectiveness is ranked in terms of the amount of displacement of the system due to impact. Standard ratings defined by the federal government define the distance the vehicle travels before it is brought to rest. The most effective systems stop the vehicles within three feet, moderately effective barriers stop the vehicle within 20 feet, and the least effective systems require up to 50 feet.

Fencing

Remember

Fencing is a common means of establishing a physical protective barrier to protect a controlled area but it should never be considered as a stand alone measure. A fence may discourage some people but it serves no purpose at all if it is breached and no-one knows about it. That is why we emphasize an integrated physical security system. If you are going to install a fence you must implement other systems such as sensors or cameras to alert you in case of intrusion. A fence within a fence is another way of reducing false alarms with sensors placed only on the inner fence.

The type of fencing used depends primarily on the threat and the degree of permanence. It may also depend on the availability of materials and the time needed for construction. Fencing may be erected for other uses besides impeding personnel access, such as obstructing views, serving as a means to defeat stand-off weapon systems (e.g., rocket-propelled grenades), and serving as a barrier to hand-thrown weapons (e.g., grenades and firebombs).

Remember

Fencing may be used to augment or increase the security of existing barriers that protect restricted areas. Examples include the creation an additional barrier line and an increase in the existing fence height. It is important to recognize that fencing provides very little delay when it comes to motivated aggressors, but it can act as a psychological deterrent when an aggressor is deciding which building to attack.

Other Perimeter Barriers

The exterior of a building may form a part of a perimeter barrier. Brick or block masonry or cast in place concrete walls may act as part of a perimeter barrier. They must be at least 7 feet high and should have a barbed wire top guard, depending on the threat and application. The windows, active doors, and other designated openings should be protected with fastening bars, grilles, or chain-link screens, and window barriers should be fastened from the inside. If hinged, the hinges and locks must be on the inside to facilitate emergency egress.

Barrier walls designed to resist the effects of an explosion can, in some cases, act to reduce the pressure levels acting on the exterior walls of buildings. They may not, however, enhance security because they prohibit observation of activities occurring on the other side of the wall. In this case, a plinth wall (anti-ram knee wall) with a fence may be an effective solution to combine anti-ram capability and observation. Consideration should also be given to the improvement of a defensive posture should threat levels increase. A number of temporary or semi-permanent measures may be effective. Expedient methods include blocking access routes with heavy vehicles or temporarily blocking roads surrounding a building to create a form of controlled access area.

Remember

Typically, street closures exclude vehicles, but allow access by pedestrians with proper credentials. The use of street closures must be balanced against minimum circulation/access requirements and fire protection considerations.

Gates and Entrances

The number of gates and perimeter entrances must be the minimum required for safe and efficient operation of the facility. Manned and active perimeter entrances must be designed so that the security force maintains full control without an unnecessary delay in traffic. This is accomplished by having sufficient entrances to accommodate the peak flow of pedestrian and vehicular traffic and having adequate lighting for rapid and efficient inspection. When necessary, install vehicle barriers in front of vehicle gates. Security lighting should be considered at entry points.

When gates are not operational during non-duty hours, they should be securely locked, illuminated during hours of darkness, and inspected periodically by a roving patrol or monitors. Additionally, warning signs should be used to warn drivers when gates are closed. Doors and windows on buildings that form a part of the perimeter should be locked, lighted, and inspected.

Semi-active entrances, such as infrequently used vehicular gates, must be locked on the inside when not in use. When closed, gates and entrances must provide a barrier structurally comparable to their associated barriers. Care must be afforded against the ability to crawl under gates. Top guards, which may be vertical, are required for all gates.

Tips

Entry Control Stations

Entry-control stations should be provided at main perimeter entrances where security personnel are present. They should be located as close as practical to the perimeter entrance to permit personnel inside the station to maintain constant surveillance over the entrance and its approaches. Additional considerations at entry-control stations include:

- ☐ Establishing a holding area for unauthorized vehicles or those to be inspected further. A turnaround area should be provided to keep from impeding other traffic.
- ☐ Establishing control measures such as displaying a decal on the window or having a specially marked vehicle.

Entry-control stations that are manned 24 hours each day should have interior and exterior lighting, interior heating (where appropriate), and a sufficient glassed area to afford adequate observation for personnel inside. Each station should also include a telephone, a radio, and badge racks (if required).

Signs should be erected to assist in controlling authorized entry, to deter unauthorized entry, and to preclude accidental entry. Signs should be plainly displayed and be legible from any approach to the perimeter from a reasonable distance. The size and coloring of a sign, its letters, and the interval of posting must be appropriate to each situation.

Entry-control stations should be hardened against attacks according to the type of threat. The methods of hardening may include—

☐ Reinforced concrete or masonry.

☐ Steel plating.

☐ Bullet-resistant glass.

☐ Sandbags, two layers in depth.

☐ Commercially fabricated, bullet-resistant building components or assemblies.

Warning Signs

A significant amount of warning signs should be erected to ensure that possible intruders are aware of entry into restricted areas. Warning signs augment control signs. They warn intruders that the area is restricted and that, depending on the type of facility involved, trespassing may result in the use of deadly force.

Warning signs should be installed along the limited area's physical barriers and at each entry point where they can be seen readily and understood by anyone approaching the perimeter.

In areas where a language other than English is also commonly spoken, warning signs should be in both languages.

Other signs

Signs setting forth the conditions of entry to an installation or area should be plainly posted at all principal entrances. The signs should be legible under normal conditions at a distance not less than 50 feet from the point of entry. Such signs should inform the entrant of the provisions (search of the person, the vehicle, packages, and so forth) or prohibitions (such as against cameras, matches, and lighters and entry for reasons other than official business) that may be prescribed by the security manager.

Physical Security Lighting

Remember Security lighting allows security personnel to maintain visual-assessment capability during darkness. When security-lighting provisions are impractical, additional security posts and/or other security means are necessary.

Security lighting should be provided wherever possible for overall site/building illumination and the perimeter to allow security personnel to maintain visual-assessment during darkness.

Security lighting provides both a real and psychological deterrent. It should not be used as a psychological deterrent only. It should also be used along perimeter fences when the situation dictates that the fence be under continuous or periodic observation.

Lighting is relatively inexpensive to maintain and, when properly used, may reduce the need for security forces. It may also enhance personal protection for forces by reducing the advantages of concealment and surprise for a determined intruder.

Security lighting is desirable for those sensitive areas or structures within the perimeter that are under observation. Such areas or structures include pier and dock areas, vital buildings, storage areas, motor pools, and vulnerable control points in communication and power- and water-distribution systems. In interior areas where night operations are conducted, adequate lighting facilitates the detection of unauthorized persons approaching or attempting malicious acts within the area. Security lighting has considerable value as a deterrent to thieves and vandals and may make the job of the saboteur more difficult. It is an essential element of an integrated physical security program.

A secure auxiliary power source and power-distribution system for the facility should be installed to provide redundancy to critical security lighting and other security equipment. During an incident, primary power may not exist or may be subject to constraints or interruptions due to poor infrastructure or hostile activity. Auxiliary power sources must be available for critical electrical loads and must be secured against direct and indirect fires as well as sabotage. If automatic-transfer switches are not installed, security procedures must designate the responsibility for the manual start of the source.

Security lighting enables security/guard-force personnel to observe activities around or inside an installation while minimizing their presence. An adequate level of illumination for all approaches to an installation will not discourage unauthorized entry; however, adequate lighting improves the ability of security personnel to assess visually and intervene on attempts at unauthorized entry. Lighting is used with other security measures (such as fixed security posts or patrols, fences, and ESSs) and should never be used alone. Other principles of security lighting include the following:
Remember

☐ Optimum security lighting is achieved by adequate, even light on bordering areas; glaring lights in the eyes of an intruder; and little light on security-patrol routes. In addition to seeing long distances, security forces must be able to see low contrasts (such as indistinct outlines of silhouettes) and must be able to detect an intruder who may be exposed to view for only a few seconds. Higher levels of illumination improve these abilities.

☐ High brightness contrast between an intruder and the background should be the first consideration when planning for security lighting. With predominantly dark, dirty surfaces or camouflage-type painted surfaces, more light is needed to produce the same brightness around installations and buildings than when clean concrete, light brick, and grass predominate. When the same amount of light falls on an object and its background, the observer must depend on contrasts in the amount of light reflected. His ability to distinguish poor contrasts is significantly improved by increasing the illumination level.

☐ The observer primarily sees an outline or a silhouette when the intruder is darker than his background. Using light finishes on the lower parts of buildings and structures may expose an intruder who depends on dark clothing and darkened face and hands. Stripes on walls have also been used effectively, as they provide recognizable breaks in outlines or silhouettes. Providing broad-lighted areas around and within the installation against which intruders can be seen can also create good observation conditions.

To be effective, two basic systems or a combination of both may be used to provide practical and effective security lighting. The first method is to light the boundaries and approaches; the second is to light the area and structures within the property's general boundaries. Protective lighting should—

☐ Discourage or deter attempts at entry by intruders. Proper illumination may lead a potential intruder to believe detection is inevitable.

☐ Make detection likely if entry is attempted.

☐ Prevent glare that may temporarily blind the guards.

Light Surveys

Before embarking on any lighting upgrades have your security consultant or an electrical engineer review your current lighting situation. For instance does it meet Department of Defense requirements which provide a good benchmark. In most cases it will not but it will point you in the direction you need to go.

Electronic Security Systems

Remember

Electronic security, including surveillance, intrusion detection, and screening, is a key element of facility protection. The purpose of electronic security is to improve the reliability and effectiveness of life safety systems, security systems, and building functions. When possible, accommodations should be made for future developments in security systems.

Checklist

Features of a good perimeter sensor system
☐ Continuous line of detection
☐ Protection in depth
☐ Complementary sensors
☐ Alarm combination and priority schemes
☐ Clear zone
☐ Sensor configuration
☐ Site-specific
☐ Tamper protection

☐ Self-test capability

☐ Suitable for physical and environmental conditions

☐ Integration with assessment system

☐ Integration with barrier delay

☐ Pattern recognition

An overall site-security system is comprised of three major sub-elements — detection, delay, and response. The detection sub-element includes intrusion detection, assessment, and entry control. An ESS is an integrated system that encompasses interior and exterior sensors; CCTV systems for assessing alarm conditions; electronic entry-control systems (EECSs); data-transmission media (DTM); and alarm reporting systems for monitoring, controlling, and displaying various alarm and system information. Interior and exterior sensors and their associated communication and display subsystems are collectively called IDSs.

Exterior Intrusion Detection Sensors

Exterior intrusion-detection sensors are customarily used to detect an intruder crossing the boundary of a protected area. They can also be used in clear zones between fences or around buildings, for protecting materials and equipment stored outdoors within a protected boundary, or in estimating the PD for buildings and other facilities.

☐ Fence sensors.

☐ Buried line sensors.

☐ LOS sensors.

☐ Video motion (video analytic) systems.

One of the problems with installing a perimeter fence with detection sensors is that a number of things such as dogs or deer can activate them. A practical way to avoid this is to install a double fence. The outermost fence has no detection sensors while the innermost fence does. It does not matter if a deer now runs into the outer fence because your concern is when something breaches this perimeter and activates the sensors on the inner fence.

Remember

Passive sensors will detect the presence of an intruder while active sensors will transmit that information to a control room or guard post to initiate a response.

There are advantages and disadvantages to covert and invisible sensors. If sensors are visible they may act as a deterrent but they can also be disabled if accessible. Invisible sensors may catch intruders unawares because they are more difficult to detect but you may lose the deterrent benefit that comes from having them visible.

Line of sight fences or barriers require flat ground because if there are hollows an intruder can hide and not be seen. Fences that follow the undulations of the terrain need sensors to detect intrusions in blind spots.

Close Circuit Television (CCTV)

Tips

A properly integrated CCTV assessment system provides a rapid and cost-effective method for determining the cause of intrusion alarms. For surveillance, a properly designed CCTV system provides a cost-effective supplement to patrols. For large facilities, the cost of a CCTV system is more easily justified. It is important to recognize that CCTV alarm assessment systems and CCTV surveillance systems perform separate and distinct functions. The alarm-assessment system is designed to respond rapidly, automatically, and predictably to the receipt of ESS alarms at the security center. The surveillance system is designed to be used at the discretion of and under the control of the security center's console operator.

When the primary function of the CCTV system is to provide real-time alarm assessment, the design should incorporate a video-processing system that can communicate with the alarm-processing system.

Video systems have become increasingly sophisticated in the last few years thanks to networking and analytical software.

Remember

Cameras act as a deterrent but are of little use unless the images they capture can be acted on immediately. Cameras that send images to video tapes that can be reviewed are of little use in detection and response. The images have to be transmitted to monitors in a control room that is manned by people who understand the need for constant vigilance and can direct appropriate response.

Network video is sometimes referred to as IP-based video surveillance or IP-surveillance. It can use a wired or wireless IP network to send digital video, audio and other data and allows video to be recorded and monitored from anywhere on the network, whether it is a local area network (LAN) or a wide area network (WAN) such as the Internet.

A network video system comprises network cameras, video encoders and video management software. Of course, there also has to be a network, storage capacity, servers and other standard IT equipment.

IP-based CCTV is similar to analog CCTV except that heavy coax cable is replaced by IP cameras on the wired or wireless network and the Internet. Video images and other information are stored on digital disks. There are still four main components – image capture, image transmission, storage and video management. However, you don't necessarily need a central security monitoring room. IP-based CCTV can be monitored anywhere on the network and that could mean at another facility completely.

Main Differences between Analog CCTV and IP CCTV

Analog CCTV	IP CCTV
Analog camera	IP camera/encoder
Analog matrix switcher	IP network switch
VCR/DVR	NVR
Coax	CAT-5
TV lines	CIF resolution
Multiplexed images per sec	Kilobits per second
CCTV keyboard	CCTV keyboard or PC

IP Security Cameras

Surveillance cameras continue to become more sophisticated and with an ever growing range of capabilities including motion activated, tilt and panning, thermal and infrared. They can be ruggedized for the toughest outdoor environment and resolution, currently around 10 Megapixel, continues to improve.

Video Surveillance

Video surveillance is like insurance, you hope you never need it but you are mighty glad to have it when you do. To be effective it has to be operational round the clock and this means alternate power sources.

Originally CCTV surveillance involved a human operator having to constantly monitor a bank of screens carrying all the camera feeds. That was labor-intensive and relied heavily on the efficiency and concentration of the security staff involved. It was quickly realized that staff needed to take breaks or handle other duties, so information was recorded on VCRs so that it could be played back. Some basic video surveillance systems still use VCRs. However, these have largely been replaced by digital video recorders (DVRs) and network video recorders (NVRs). The advantage of DVRs is that they can be accessed from any PC or laptop. The challenge for IT and security staff is that this 24/7 monitoring generates huge volumes of streaming information which has to be stored and then quickly accessed when necessary. Servers and file system organization enable the data to be stored – often requiring terabytes and even petabytes of storage - and one way to overcome the problem of monitoring more data is to use video management (VM) technology coupled with behavioral analytic software. VM software controls the IP cameras, records the information and using intelligent software, is programed to decide what to display on the monitor for the human operator to see. This system allows the use of many more cameras, if needed, but less, although more highly-trained monitoring staff.

Video Motion Sensors

A video motion sensor generates an alarm when an intruder enters or when detected activity occurs within a selected portion of a CCTV camera's field of view. The problem is that the cause of the alarm may not be immediately apparent and this has usually required human intervention to monitor a screen and determine what action, if any, needs to be taken under laid down protocols. Rules-based technologies take this a step further and look for specific warning signs or events before triggering an alert. However, writing these programs requires considerable expertise and every time a new warning sign needs to be entered into the system, a new program has to be written.

Behavioral analytics mentioned above, provides actionable intelligence. This technique examines observational data. When observations are identified that cannot be explained, the system can both alert the human operator and learn from the data, automatically building up an ever expanding behavioral library.

Boundary Penetration Sensors

Boundary-penetration sensors are designed to detect penetration or attempted penetration through perimeter barriers. These barriers include walls, ceilings, duct openings, doors, and windows.

Structural-Vibration Sensors

Structural-vibration sensors detect low-frequency energy generated in an attempted penetration of a physical barrier (such as a wall or a ceiling) by hammering, drilling, cutting, detonating explosives, or employing other forcible methods of entry.

Glass-Breakage Sensors

Glass-breakage sensors detect the breaking of glass. The noise from breaking glass consists of frequencies in both the audible and ultrasonic range. Glass-breakage sensors use microphone transducers to detect the glass breakage.

Passive Ultrasonic Sensors

Passive ultrasonic sensors detect acoustical energy in the ultrasonic frequency range, typically between 20 and 30 kilohertz (kHz). They are used to detect an attempted penetration through rigid barriers (such as metal or masonry walls, ceilings, and floors). They also detect penetration through windows and vents covered by metal grilles, shutters, or bars if these openings are properly sealed against outside sounds.

Balanced Magnetic Switches. Balanced magnetic switches (BMSs) are typically used to detect the opening of a door. These sensors can also be used on windows, hatches, gates, or other structural devices that can be opened to gain entry.

Grid-Wire Sensors

The grid-wire sensor consists of a continuous electrical wire arranged in a grid pattern. The wire maintains an electrical current. An alarm is generated when the wire is broken. The sensor detects forced entry through walls, floors, ceilings, doors, windows, and other barriers.

Volumetric Motion Sensors

Volumetric motion sensors are designed to detect intruder motion within the interior of a protected volume. Volumetric sensors may be active or passive. Active sensors (such as microwave) fill the volume to be protected with an energy pattern and recognize a disturbance in the pattern when anything moves within the detection zone.

Microwave Motion Sensors

With microwave motion sensors, high-frequency electromagnetic energy is used to detect an intruder's motion within the protected area.

PIR Motion Sensors

PIR motion sensors detect a change in the thermal energy pattern caused by a moving intruder and initiate an alarm when the change in energy satisfies the detector's alarm criteria. These sensors are passive devices because they do not transmit energy; they monitor the energy radiated by the surrounding environment.

Dual-Technology Sensors

To minimize the generation of alarms caused by sources other than intruders, dual-technology sensors combine two different technologies in one unit. Ideally, this is achieved by combining two sensors that individually have a high PD and do not respond to common sources of false alarms. Available dual-technology sensors combine an active ultrasonic or microwave sensor with a PIR sensor.

Point Sensors

Point sensors are used to protect specific objects within a facility. These sensors (sometimes referred to as proximity sensors) detect an intruder coming in close proximity to, touching, or lifting an object.

Pressure Mats

Pressure mats generate an alarm when pressure is applied to any part of the mat's surface, as when someone steps on the mat.

Site Utilities

Remember

Utility systems can suffer significant damage when subjected to the shock of an explosion. Some of these utilities may be critical for safely evacuating people from the building. Their destruction could cause damage that is disproportionate to other building damage resulting from an explosion. To minimize the possibility of such hazards, apply the following measures:

Checklist

☐ Where possible, provide underground, concealed, and protected utilities.

☐ Provide redundant utility systems to support site security, life safety, and rescue functions.

☐ Consider quick connects for portable utility backup systems if redundant sources are not available.

☐ Prepare vulnerability assessments for all utility services to the site, including all utility lines, storm sewers, gas transmission lines, electricity transmission lines, and other utilities that may cross the site perimeter.

☐ Protect water treatment plants and storage tanks from waterborne contaminants by securing access points, such as manholes. Maintain routine water testing to help detect waterborne contaminants.

☐ Minimize signs identifying critical utility complexes (e.g., power plants and water treatment plants). Provide fencing to prevent unauthorized access and use landscape planting to conceal aboveground systems.

☐ Locate petroleum, oil, and lubricant storage tanks and operations buildings downslope from all other buildings. Site fuel tanks at an elevation lower than operational buildings or utility plants. Locate fuel storage tanks at least 100 feet from buildings.

☐ Locate the main fuel storage away from loading docks, entrances, and parking. Access should be restricted and protected (e.g., locks on caps and seals).

☐ Provide utility systems with redundant or loop service, particularly in the case of electrical systems. Where more than one source or service is not currently available, provisions should be made for future connections. In the interim, consider "quick connects" at the building for portable backup systems.

☐ Decentralize a site's communications resources when possible; the use of multiple communications networks will strengthen the communications system's ability to withstand the effects of a terrorist attack. Careful consideration should be made in locating, concealing, and protecting key network resources such as network control centers.

☐ Place trash receptacles as far away from the building as possible; trash receptacles should not be placed within 30 feet of a building.

☐ Conceal incoming utility systems within building and property lines, and give them blast protection, including burial or proper encasement, wherever possible.

☐ Consider incorporating low impact development practices to enhance security, such as retaining stormwater on site in a pond to create stand-off, instead of sending into the sewer system.

☐ Locate utility systems at least 50 feet from loading docks, front entrances, and parking areas.

☐ Route critical or fragile utilities so that they are not on exterior walls or on walls shared with mailrooms.

☐ Where redundant utilities are required in accordance with other requirements or criteria, ensure that the redundant utilities are not collocated or do not run in the same chases. This minimizes the possibility that both sets of utilities will be adversely affected by a single event.

☐ Where emergency backup systems are required, ensure they are located away from the systems components for which they provide backup.

☐ Mount all overhead utilities and other fixtures weighing 31 pounds (14 kilograms) or more to minimize the likelihood that they will fall and injure building occupants. Design all equipment mountings to resist forces of 0.5 times the equipment weight in any direction and 1.5 times the equipment weight in the downward direction. This standard does not preclude the need to design equipment mountings for forces required by other criteria such as seismic standards.

☐ To limit opportunities for aggressors placing explosives underneath buildings, ensure that access to crawl spaces, utility tunnels, and other means of under building access is controlled. All utility penetrations of a site's perimeter barrier, including penetrations in fences, walls, or other perimeter structures, should be sealed or secured to eliminate openings large enough to pass through the barrier. Typical penetrations could be for storm sewers, water, electricity, or other site utility services.

☐ All utility penetrations of the site's perimeter should be screened, sealed, or secured to prevent their use as access points for unauthorized entry into the site. If access is required for maintenance of utilities, secure all penetrations with screening, grating, latticework, or other similar devices so that openings do not allow intruder access. Provide intrusion detection sensors and consider overt or covert visual surveillance systems if warranted by the sensitivity of assets requiring protection.

☐ Drainage ditches, culverts, vents, ducts, and other openings that pass through a perimeter and that have a cross-sectional area greater than 96 square inches and whose smallest dimension is greater than 6 inches should be protected by securely fastened welded bar grilles. As an alternative, drainage structures may be constructed of multiple pipes, with each pipe having a diameter of 10 inches or less. Multiple pipes of this diameter may also be placed and secured in the inflow end of a drainage culvert to prevent intrusion into the area. Ensure that any addition of grills or pipes to culverts or other drainage structures is coordinated with the engineers so that they can compensate for the diminished flow capacity and additional maintenance that will result from the installation.

☐ Manhole covers 10 inches or more in diameter must be secured to prevent unauthorized opening. They may be secured with locks and hasps, by welding them shut, or by bolting them to their frame. Ensure that hasps, locks, and bolts are made of materials that resist corrosion. Keyed bolts (which make removal by unauthorized personnel more difficult) are also available. If very high security is required, manhole covers that resist shattering after being artificially "frozen" by an aggressor should be considered.

Vehicles

Control and monitoring of vehicles in and around a facility is an important and integral part of your physical security planning. You need to know where staff and visitors park and how they then access the building; where delivery vehicles park to unload and pick up; traffic flows and pedestrian patterns in the area and how these impact on each other and your facility and so on.

Your physical security planning is even more critical if you are protecting an urban facility because vehicles probably circulate on public roads around your building and may be able to park alongside it.

Must Do

If you are a high risk target terrorists could try to ram a truck containing explosives into your building. If you are in a densely populated area – near a train or bus terminus or surrounded by offices - terrorists might leave a car bomb in the street outside your building in order to cause maximum pedestrian casualties. In either case, the possibility has to be considered and the appropriate actions taken.

When designing your vehicle security planning you must also take into account the implications this may have on emergency vehicles and their ability to get to you quickly and be able to operate efficiently on arrival i.e. bollards erected along the perimeter may impede fire trucks and equipment. Uneven surfaces may slow down approaching vehicles but may pose a hazard to pedestrians and cyclists. High curbs and berms might hinder snow clearing or lead to flooding.

Loading Docks and Service Access

Remember

Loading docks and service access areas are commonly required for a building and are typically desired to be kept as invisible as possible. For this reason, special attention should be devoted to these service areas in order to avoid undesirable intruders.

Parking

If you have an extensive controlled perimeter you can better control access and with the appropriate security measures you should be able to prevent penetration by a truck or car bomb. If a truck does try to ram a perimeter barrier and explodes on impact, the stand off distance – the distance between the point of explosion and the nearest buildings inside the perimeter - should be great enough to minimize the effects of the blast.

In urban environments this is more difficult as space is at a premium and people may be parking on the streets alongside your building. The minimum standoff for all new buildings regardless of hardening is 10 meters (33 feet) for both parking areas and roadways. The Department of Defense stand-off guidelines have largely been adopted as the de facto industry standard.

For existing buildings the advice is that wherever possible, relocate parking and roadways to provide the appropriate standoff distance or retrofit the building to strengthen it.

In most cases, however, this is not practical and the following measures should be considered.

☐ **Parking Areas.** Establish access control to portions of parking areas that are closer than the required standoff distance to ensure unauthorized vehicles are not allowed closer than the required standoff distance. Controlled parking may be allowed closer if it can be shown by analysis that the required level of protection can be provided at the lesser standoff distance or if it can be provided through building hardening or other mitigating construction or retrofit.

☐ **Parking on Roadways.** Eliminate parking on roadways within the required standoff distances along roads adjacent to existing buildings covered by these standards.

Parking Facilities

There are three primary types of parking facilities, all of which present security trade-offs. Surface lots can be designed to keep vehicles away from buildings, but they consume large amounts of land and, if constructed of impervious materials, can contribute greatly to stormwater runoff volume. They can also be hazardous for pedestrians if dedicated pedestrian pathways are not provided. In contrast, on-street parking is often convenient for users and a source of revenue for local governments, but this type of parking may provide little or no setback. Finally, garage structures provide revenue and can be convenient for users, but they may require structural measures to ensure blast resistance as well as crime prevention measures to prevent street crime.

Note: When considering security, permanent fixes are not always the best solution. If your facility holds an open day once a year there is no point spending large sums of money on erecting permanent barriers to manage traffic flow for just this occasion. Rent-a-fence is a much better and much cheaper option. Again, rather than add costly, permanent measures, develop procedures that allow temporary measures.

Remember

Options

When determining whether secured and unsecured areas are adjacent to one another, consider the layout on each floor and the relationship between floors. Secured occupied or critical areas should not be placed above or below unsecured areas.

Must Do

Adequate queuing areas should be provided in front of lobby inspection stations so that visitors are not forced to stand outside during bad weather conditions or in a congested line inside a small lobby while waiting to enter the secured areas. Occupied areas or emergency functions should not be placed immediately adjacent to the lobby, but should be separated by a buffer area such as a storage area or corridor.

The interior wall area and exposed structural columns in unsecured lobby areas should be minimized.

Vehicular queuing and inspection stations need to be accounted for in design/operation of the loading docks and vehicle access points. These should be located outside the building along the curb or further away. A parking lane may be used for this purpose.

Emergency functions and elevator shafts are to be placed away from internal parking areas, loading docks and other high-risk areas. In the 1993 World Trade Center bombing incident, elevator shafts became chimneys, transmitting smoke and heat from the explosion in the basement to all levels of the building. This hindered evacuation and resulted in smoke inhalation injuries.

False ceilings, light fixtures, Venetian blinds, ductwork, air conditioners, and other nonstructural components may become flying debris in the event of an explosion. Wherever possible it is recommended that the design be simplified to limit these hazards. Placing heavy equipment such as air conditioners near the floor rather than the ceiling is one idea for limiting this hazard. Using fabric curtains or plastic vertical blinds rather than metal Venetian blinds, and using exposed ductwork as an architectural device are other ideas. Mechanically attaching light fixtures to the slab above as is done in high seismic areas is recommended.

Remember
Finally, the placement of furniture can have an effect on injury levels. Desks, conference tables, and other similar furniture should be placed as far from exterior windows facing streets as practical. Desks with computer monitors should be oriented away from the window to prevent injury due to the impact of the monitor.

People

As you can see, various components need to be incorporated into the plan. The most important of these is people – the people employed in the facility, visitors to it, security staff, people in the wider community and so on. You cannot develop a valid PPS without taking people into account and you cannot implement it effectively without their support.

Must Do
This raises a number of technical issues. People have to be educated about the new procedures systems, trained to use them and get comfortable with them and this can raise sensitive issues. For instance, you may install turnstiles and then face issues with some members of staff who cannot use them either because of disabilities or because of a weight problem. Security managers are not people friendly so human resources and other departments have to be involved in the process. Ultimately no integrated physical security will work unless the people it is meant to protect are behind it.

It is important when developing your plan to have a clear understanding of who your employees are and that should even include their habits – for instance, whether they smoke or not. Do you have to incorporate smoking areas outside the building to accommodate them? This is better than having them sneak outside through an emergency door and setting off alarms around the building. The danger is that if this happens on a regular basis, security will assume that someone has gone outside to have a cigarette again when, in fact, there could have been a serious security breach.

Remember
Effective security requires technology and people to work together to implement policies, processes, and procedures that serve as countermeasures to identified risks.

To illustrate this point, let us examine the following scenario: an organization has policies in place to mitigate the risk of an outsider committing a harmful act against its employees. One policy states that entry to the building is restricted to authorized personnel and another that no weapons may be brought into the building. An access control system implements the first policy by requiring that people wishing to enter present a smart card with a biometric that matches the stored biometric of the authorized person. A detection system implements the second policy by requiring people to pass through a metal detection portal and their belongings to be scanned by an x-ray machine. These procedures ensure compliance with the policies. However, to be effective, security personnel must enforce the policies by following the prescribed procedures. If security personnel allow exceptions to these procedures, they are failing to enforce compliance with the policies. Just as damaging is the lack of effective security processes. For example, if there are no processes in place to handle the entry of employees who have forgotten their identity access cards, a vulnerability may be created that could be exploited by adversaries.

Breaches in security resulting from human error are more likely to occur if personnel do not understand the risks and the policies that are put in place to mitigate them. Training is essential to successfully implementing policies by ensuring that personnel exercise good judgment in following security procedures. In addition, having the best available security technology cannot ensure protection if people have not been trained in how to use it properly. Training is particularly essential if the technology requires personnel to master certain knowledge and skills to operate it.

Must Do

For example, x-ray inspection systems rely heavily on the operator to detect concealed objects in the generated x-ray images. If security personnel have not received adequate training in understanding how the technology works and detecting threat images, such as a knife, the security system will be much less effective.

There is a difference between screening people and the objects they have with them. You may be able to go through the carousel with a laptop bag but what if you have just flown back from a trip and have a wheeled suitcase that is too large to go through the gate – and it is an unmanned entry point? One solution is to have a phone so that you can call someone to escort you in.

Privacy Issues

Remember

Balancing the needs for security and respecting the privacy of staff has always been a difficult issue. An employee has legal and regulatory obligations and must ensure that security systems and processes do not infringe these laws. Equally they have a duty to do everything they can to protect staff and visitors to their facility.

Staff have a "reasonable expectation of privacy" and this prevents monitoring areas such as restrooms and changing rooms. This does not necessarily extend to their use of computers and staff phones.

Employers also have to be sensitive to the needs of all staff. For instance, special accommodations have to be made for the disabled – for instance, wheelchair bound or blind workers – as well as larger-than-average employees who may have difficulty going through entrance security carousel and so on.

Employee Screening

Must Do

Screening job applicants to eliminate security risks is important and personnel screenings should be incorporated into standard personnel policies. An applicant should be required to complete a personnel security questionnaire, which is then screened for completeness and used to eliminate undesirable applicants. A careful investigation should be conducted to ensure that the applicant's character, associations, and suitability for employment are satisfactory. The following sources may be helpful in securing employment investigative data:

- ☐ State and local police (including national and local police in overseas areas).
- ☐ Former employers.
- ☐ Public records.
- ☐ Credit agencies.
- ☐ Schools (all levels).
- ☐ References. (These references should include those names not furnished by the applicant. These are known as throw offs, and they are obtained during interviews of references furnished by applicants.)

Security Staff

As already illustrated, regardless of the use of structural, mechanical, or electronic equipment, the human element in security operations makes the difference between success and failure. Personnel who perform physical-security duties must be disciplined and alert, have sound judgment, be confident and physically fit, and possess good interpersonal communication skills.

Tips

Security staff are part of your response and so they need to be involved in the design and Gap Closure phases , and especially the deter and detect elements. In order to respond effectively they need to know what is in front of them and behind them.

Security personnel must exercise good interpersonal communication skills when carrying out their duties with other employees. Bad employee relations can result if security personnel become impertinent and assume powers not rightfully theirs. Security personnel must understand the methods and techniques that will detect security hazards and assist in identifying violators and intruders.

Written reports or journals are recommended for security activities. These reports should record all activities, actions, and visits at the security post.

The extent and type of training required for security personnel will vary according to the importance, vulnerability, size, and other factors affecting a particular installation or facility. The training program's objective is to ensure that all personnel are able to perform routine and emergency duties competently and efficiently.

Efficient and continuing training is the most effective means of obtaining and maintaining maximum proficiency of security personnel. Regardless of the selection process, new personnel seldom have all of the qualifications and experience necessary to do the job. In addition, new or revised job requirements frequently mean that personnel must be retrained. Training can bridge the void between ability and job requirement.

A good training program helps to instill confidence through developing increased skill proficiency. The training program provides for more flexibility and better physical protection, fewer required personnel, and less time to learn duties.

Testing designed to evaluate performance is a necessary step in the training program. These tests may be oral or written or may be a type of performance test. They should be administered annually to ensure that the entire force maintains high standards of proficiency. A testing program also helps to improve training by—

☐ Discovering gaps in learning.

☐ Emphasizing main points.

☐ Evaluating instructional methods

A security force is the critical element of a successful physical-security program. It is as strong as its weakest member. A comprehensive training program is essential to a knowledgeable, disciplined, and alert security force. A well-trained security force will be prepared to respond to a security breach.

Remember

Lock and Key Systems

Locks are the most acceptable and widely used security devices for protecting facilities, classified materials, and property. All containers, rooms, and facilities must be locked when not in actual use. Regardless of their quality or cost, locks are considered delay devices only. Some locks require considerable time and expert manipulation to open, but all locks can be defeated by force and with the proper tools. Locks must never be considered as a stand-alone method of security.

Key Locks

Key locks consist of, but are not limited to, the following:

☐ Cylindrical locksets are often called key-in-knob or key-in-lever locks. They are normally used to secure offices and storerooms. The locking cylinder located in the center of the doorknob distinguishes these locks. Some cylindrical locksets have keyways in each of the opposing knobs that require a key on either side to lock and unlock them. Others unlock with a key, but may be locked by pushing or rotating a button on the inside knob. These locks are suitable only for very low-security applications. Using these locks may require compensatory measures in the form of additional locks on containers within the room.

☐ Dead-bolt locks are sometimes called tubular dead bolts. They are mounted on the door in a manner similar to cylindrical locksets. The primary difference is in the bolt. When the bolt is extended (locked), the dead bolt projects into the doorframe at least one inch, and it cannot be forced back (unlocked) by applying pressure to the end of the bolt. The dead-bolt lock has the potential for providing acceptable levels of protection for storerooms and other areas where more security is desired. It is recommended for use in military housing as an effective security measure in the installation's crime-prevention program. In situations where there is a window in or adjacent to the door, a double cylinder dead-bolt lock (one that requires a key to open from either side) should be used.

☐ Mortise locks are so named because the lock case is mortised or recessed into the edge of the door. The most common variety of mortise locks has a doorknob on each side of the door. Entrance doors often have an exterior thumb latch rather than a doorknob. The mortise lock can be locked from inside by means of a thumb turn or by a button. Mortise locks are considered low-security devices since they weaken the door in the mortised area.

☐ Drop-bolt locks (often referred to as jimmy-proof locks) are normally used as auxiliary locks similar to dead bolts. Both the drop-bolt lock body and the strike have interlocking leaves similar to a door hinge. When closed, locking pins in the lock body drop down into the holes provided in the strike and secure the locking system. Since the lock body and the strike are interconnected with locking pins when closed, the lock essentially becomes a single unit and is extremely difficult to separate.

☐ Rim-cylinder locks are mounted to the door's inside surface and are secured by screws in the door face. These locks are generally used with drop-bolt and other surface-mounted locks and latches. They consist of an outer barrel, a cylinder and ring, a tailpiece, a back mounting plate, and two mounting screws. The tailpiece screws are usually scored so that the lock can be tailored to fit varying door thicknesses.

☐ Unit locks are ideal in heavily traveled facilities (such as hospitals or institutional buildings). These locks are a complete, one-piece unit that slides into a notch cut into the door's latch edge. The one-size cutout of the door edge simplifies the door preparation for the lock.

☐ Mechanical, push-button combination locks are digital (push buttons numbered 1 through 9) combination door-locking devices used to deny area access to any individual not authorized or cleared for a specific area. These locks are normally used for access control and should be backed up by door locking devices when the facility is unoccupied.

☐ Padlocks are detachable locks that are typically used with a hasp. Low security padlocks, sometimes called secondary padlocks, are used to deter unauthorized access, and they provide only minimal resistance to force. Low-security locks are made with hardened steel shackles. Precautions must be taken to avoid confusing these locks with similar brass or bronze locks. The brass or bronze locks are commonly used but do not meet the security requirements of the hardened shackled locks. High-security padlocks provide the maximum resistance to unauthorized entry when used with a high security hasp.

Combination Locks

Combination locks are available as padlocks or as mounted locks. They are low-security padlocks with combinations that are either fixed or changeable.

Access Barriers

Turnstiles and revolving doors are access barriers that can be installed to continuously control and monitor every individual entering and or exiting a building. Whereas revolving doors are most often deployed to control the entry to a building from the street, turnstiles are usually set within the lobby of a building.

Electronic Entry Control

The function of an entry control system is to ensure that only authorized personnel are permitted into or out of a controlled area. Entry can be controlled by locked fence gates, locked doors to a building or rooms within a building, or specially designed portals. Devices include swipe cards and key pads.

Proximity cards contain an embedded antenna that sends out a low level fixed radio frequency signal. They can be used to open secured doors and turnstiles. The disadvantage is that possession of the card does not guarantee that it is being used by the person it was assigned to.

Note: A growing trend is for companies to use their logos on entry cards but this should be discouraged. If a bad guy finds a card that has been lost, they immediately know where to go to gain access. There is, however, no problem in using the company logo on temporary visitor cards which never leave the building.

Remember

Identification Systems

An ID system provides a method of identifying personnel. The system provides for personal recognition and the use of security ID cards or badges to aid in the control and movement of personnel activities.

Standard ID cards are generally acceptable for access into areas that are unrestricted and have no security interest. Personnel requiring access to restricted areas should be issued a security ID card or badge.

Four of the most commonly used access-control ID methods are the personal-recognition system, the single-card or -badge system, the card- or badge-exchange system, and the multiple-card or -badge system.

Personal-Recognition System

The personal-recognition system is the simplest of all systems. A member of the security force providing access control visually checks the person requesting entry. Entry is granted based on—

☐ The individual being recognized.

☐ The need to enter has been established.

☐ The person is on an access-control roster.

Single-Card or -Badge System

This system reflects permission to enter specific areas by the badge depicting specific letters, numbers, or particular colors. This system lends to comparatively loose control and is not recommended for high-security areas. Permission to enter specific areas does not always go with the need to know. Because the ID cards/badges frequently remain in the bearer's possession while off duty, it affords the opportunity for alteration or duplication.

Card- or Badge-Exchange System

In this system, two cards/badges contain identical photographs. Each card/badge has a different background color, or one card/badge has an overprint. One card/badge is presented at the entrance to a specific area and exchanged for the second card/badge, which is worn or carried while in that area. Individual possession of the second card/badge occurs only while the bearer is in the area for which it was issued. When leaving the area, the second card/badge is returned and maintained in the security area. This method provides a greater degree of security and decreases the possibility of forgery, alteration, or duplication of the card/badge.

Multiple-Card or -Badge System

This system provides the greatest degree of security. Instead of having specific markings on the cards/badges denoting permission to enter various restricted areas, the multiple card/badge system makes an exchange at the entrance to each security area. The card/badge information is identical and allows for comparisons. Exchange cards/badges are maintained at each area only for individuals who have access to the specific area.

Mechanized/Automated Systems

An alternative to using security personnel to visually check cards/badges and access rosters is to use building card-access systems or biometric-access readers. These systems can control the flow of personnel entering and exiting a complex.

Included in these systems are—

☐ Coded devices such as mechanical or electronic keypads or combination locks.

☐ Credential devices such as magnetic-strip or proximity card readers.

☐ Biometric devices such as fingerprint readers or retina scanners.

Access-control and ID systems base their judgment factor on a remote capability through a routine discriminating device for positive ID. These systems do not require security staff at entry points; they identify an individual in the following manner:

☐ The system receives physical ID data from an individual.

☐ The data is encoded and compared to stored information.

☐ The system determines whether access is authorized.

☐ The information is translated into readable results.

Specialized mechanical systems are ideal for highly sensitive situations because they use a controlled process in a controlled environment to establish the required database and accuracy. One innovative technique applied to ID and admittance procedures involves dimension comparisons. The dimension of a person's full hand is compared to previously stored data to determine entry authorization. Other specialized machine readers can scan a single fingerprint or an eye retina and provide positive ID of anyone attempting entry.

An all-inclusive automated ID and access-control system reinforces the security in-depth ring through its easy and rapid change capability. The computer is able to do this through its memory. Changes can be made quickly by the system's administrator.

Remember

The commercial security market has a wide range of mechanized and automated hardware and software systems. Automated equipment is chosen only after considering the security needs and the environment in which it operates. These considerations include whether the equipment is outdoors or indoors, the temperature range, and weather conditions. Assessment of security needs and the use of planning, programming, and budgeting procedures greatly assist a security manager in improving the security posture.

Card/badge specifications

Upon issuing a card/badge, security personnel must explain to the bearer the wear required and the authorizations allowed with the card/badge. This includes—

☐ Designation of the areas where an ID card/badge is required.

☐ A description of the type of card/badge in use and the authorizations and limitations placed on the bearer.

☐ The required presentation of the card/badge when entering or leaving each area during all hours of the day.

☐ Details of when, where, and how the card/badge should be worn, displayed, or carried.

☐ Procedures to follow in case of loss or damage of the card.

☐ The disposition of the card/badge upon termination of employment, investigations, or personnel actions.

☐ Prerequisites for reissuing the card/badge.

Visitor IDs and Controls

Must Do Procedures must be implemented to properly identify and control personnel. This includes visitors presenting their cards/badges to security at entrances of restricted areas. Visitors are required to stay with their assigned escort. Security must ensure that visitors stay in areas relating to their visit; an uncontrolled visitor, although conspicuously identified, could acquire information for which he is not authorized.

Physical-security precautions against pilferage, espionage, and sabotage require the screening, ID, and control of visitors. Visitors are generally classed in the following categories:

☐ Persons with whom every installation or facility has business (such as suppliers, customers, insurance inspectors, and government inspectors).

☐ Individuals or groups who desire to visit an installation or facility for personal or educational reasons. Such visits may be desired by educational, technical, or scientific organizations.

☐ Individuals or groups specifically sponsored by the government (such as foreign nationals visiting under technical cooperation programs and similar visits by US nationals).

☐ Guided tours to selected portions of the installation in the interest of public relations.

The ID and control mechanisms for visitors must be in place. They may include the following:

☐ Methods of establishing the authority for admitting visitors and any limitations relative to access.

☐ Positive ID of visitors by personal recognition, visitor permit, or other identifying credentials. Contact the employer, supervisor, or officer in charge to validate the visit.

☐ The use of visitor registration forms. These forms provide a record of the visitor and the time, location, and duration of his visit.

☐ The use of visitor ID cards/badges. The cards/badges bear serial numbers, the area or areas to which access is authorized, the bearer's name, and escort requirements.

☐ For sensitive facilities, have a policy where visitors must call ahead prior to their arrival.

Tips Note. If your facility is sensitive and receives a lot of deliveries it is a good idea to institute a policy whereby information is sent ahead of time about the driver, the vehicle and its contents. The driver information should include a photograph so that the security staff can ensure that the right person is driving the vehicle – and not someone who has hijacked the vehicle and packed it with explosives.

Smart Cards

Smart cards, about the size and shape of a credit card, are used in access control systems to verify that the cardholder is the person he or she claims to be. They are increasingly used in one-to-one verification applications that compare a user's biometric (commonly a fingerprint or hand geometry) to the biometric template stored on the smart card. The Transportation Security Administration (TSA) requires all individuals wanting to access the nation's maritime transportation system to have Transportation Worker Identification Credentials (TWIC). The TWIC smart cards are required not only by people employed in the ports but all drivers and others accessing them for whatever reason. The cards are tamper-resistant biometric credentials.

Smart cards have several other advantages. They can hold a person's medical history which could be life-saving if you were involved in a serious accident. The cards can also be used in lieu of cash. You transfer a specific sum of money to the smart card and it can then be used in vending machines and so on. When the balance starts to run low, you top it up.

Note: Security cards and badges are now very sophisticated and enable enhanced security both for accessing the facility and while in it. Visitor cards, for instance, can change color after a specified period of time, to alert staff and security personnel that someone may have overstayed their visit. Cards and badges can allow authorized personnel to enter sensitive areas while preventing non-authorized personnel from doing so. However when greater security is needed a general rule is to have both a card and an additional form of entry check available for added protection. This additional check could be a biometric access device.

Tips

Biometric Access Controls

Biometrics are automated methods for recognizing a person based on a physiological or behavioral characteristic.

Methods most commonly used are:

☐ Fingerprint scan technology (also known as fingerprint recognition) uses the impressions made by the unique, minute, ridge formations or patterns found on the fingertips. Although fingerprint patterns may be similar, no two fingerprints have ever been found to contain identical individual ridge characteristics.

☐ Hand (or finger) geometry is based on the premise that each individual's hands, although changing over time, remain characteristically the same. The technology collects over 90 automated measurements of many dimensions of the hand and fingers, using such metrics as the height of the fingers, distance between joints, and shape of the knuckles.

☐ Retina scan technology is based on the patterns of blood vessels on the retina, a thin nerve about 1/50th of an inch thick located on the back of the eye. These patterns are unique from person to person. No two retinas are alike, not even in identical twins. Retinal patterns remain constant throughout a person's lifetime except in cases of certain diseases.

☐ Iris scan technology is based on the unique visible characteristics of the eye's iris, the colored ring that surrounds the pupil. The iris of each eye is different; even identical twins have different iris patterns. The iris remains constant over a person's lifetime. Even medical procedures such as refractive surgery, cataract surgery, and cornea transplants do not change the iris's characteristics.

☐ Facial recognition is a biometric technology that identifies people based on their facial features. Systems using this technology capture facial images from video cameras and generate templates for comparing a live facial scan of an individual to a stored template.

☐ Speaker verification works by creating a voice template based on the unique characteristics of an individual's vocal tract, which results in differences in the cadence, pitch, and tone of an individual's voice. Signature recognition authenticates the identity of individuals by measuring their handwritten signatures. The signature is treated as a series of movements that contain unique biometric data, such as personal rhythm, acceleration, and pressure flow.

Enforcement Measures

Must Do — The most vulnerable link in any ID system is its enforcement. Security forces must be proactive in performing their duties i.e. a guard who spends his feet up on the desk with his head buried in a newspaper is not going to be effective. If he doesn't know what is going on, he cannot respond.

Positive enforcement measures must be prescribed to enhance security. Some of these measures may include—

Designating alert and tactful security personnel at entry control points.

☐ Ensuring that personnel possess quick perception and good judgment.

☐ Requiring entry-control personnel to conduct frequent irregular checks of their assigned areas.

☐ Formalizing standard procedures for conducting guard mounts and posting and relieving security personnel. These measures will prevent posting of unqualified personnel and a routine performance of duty.

☐ Prescribing a uniform method of handling or wearing security ID cards/badges. If carried on the person, the card must be removed from the wallet (or other holder) and handed to security personnel. When worn, the badge will be worn in a conspicuous position to expedite inspection and recognition from a distance.

☐ Designing entry and exit control points of restricted areas to force personnel to pass in a single file in front of security personnel. In some instances, the use of turnstiles may be advisable to assist in maintaining positive control.

☐ Providing lighting at control points. The lighting must illuminate the area to enable security personnel to compare the bearer with the ID card/badge.

☐ Enforcing access-control measures by educating security forces and employees. Enforcement of access-control systems rests primarily with the security forces; however, it is essential that they have the full cooperation of the employees. Employees must be instructed to consider each unidentified or improperly identified individual as a trespasser. In restricted areas where access is limited to a particular zone, employees must report unauthorized individuals to the security force.

☐ Positioning ID card/badge racks or containers at entry control points so that they are accessible only to guard-force personnel.

☐ Appointing a responsible custodian to accomplish control procedures of cards/badges. The custodian is responsible for the issue, turn in, recovery, and renewal of security ID cards/badges.

The degree of compromise tolerable in the ID system is in direct proportion to the degree of security required. The following control procedures are recommended for preserving the integrity of a card/badge system:

☐ Maintenance of an accurate written record or log listing (by serial number) all cards and badges and showing those on hand, to whom they are issued, and their disposition (lost, mutilated, or destroyed).

☐ Authentication of records and logs by the custodian.

☐ A periodic inventory of records by a commissioned officer.

☐ The prompt invalidation of lost cards/badges.

☐ The conspicuous posting at security control points of current lists of lost or invalidated cards/badges.

☐ The establishment of controls within restricted areas to enable security personnel to determine the number of persons within the area.

☐ The establishment of the two-person rule (when required).

☐ The establishment of procedures to control the movement of visitors. A visitor-control record will be maintained and located at entry control points.

Duress Code

Tips

The duress code is designed to protect non security personnel. If people see something suspicious, they must be trained to alert the proper authorities and not try to intervene themselves which could put them and others in danger. For instance, a teacher who sees a stranger armed with a gun in the parking lot should not try to tackle the man but should use the duress code to summon help as quickly as possible.

The duress code is a simple word or phrase used during normal conversation to alert other security personnel that an authorized person is under duress. A duress code requires planning and rehearsal to ensure an appropriate response. This code is changed frequently to minimize compromise.

Two-Person Rule

Tips

The two-person rule is designed to prohibit access to sensitive areas or equipment by a lone individual. Two authorized persons are considered present when they are in a physical position from which they can positively detect incorrect or unauthorized procedures with respect to the task or operation being performed. The team is familiar with applicable safety and access to sensitive areas or equipment that requires the two-person rule. When application of the two-person rule is required, it is enforced constantly by the personnel who constitute the team.

The two-person rule is applied in many other aspects of physical security operations, such as the following:

- ❑ When uncontrolled access to vital machinery, equipment, or materiel might provide opportunity for intentional or unintentional damage that could affect the installation's mission or operation.
- ❑ When uncontrolled access to funds could provide opportunity for diversion by falsification of accounts.
- ❑ When uncontrolled delivery or receipt for materials could provide opportunity for pilferage through "short" deliveries and false receipts.
- ❑ When access to a sensitive area could provide an opportunity for theft. Keys should be issued so that at least two people must be present to unlock the locks.

Note: A facility is at its most vulnerable during an emergency so even greater awareness is needed at this time. For instance, the fire alarm has sounded and managers are overseeing an orderly evacuation of the building. However, did someone deliberately set off the alarm to gain access to a sensitive area as everyone else is leaving? Do you have procedures to cover this.

Detection Systems

Detection systems provide a second layer of security. Portal (walkthrough) metal detectors can be strategically deployed at entry control points to screen individuals for hidden firearms and other potentially injurious objects, such as knives and explosive devices, as they clear the access control system. Unlike more traditional detectors which simply generated an alarm when a metal target was detected anywhere on an individual's body, more technologically advanced portal scanners now come equipped with light bars to highlight the locations where highest metal concentrations are detected. More sensitive and ergonomic handheld detector wands are also now commercially available to perform thorough and rapid follow-up screens.

Explosive Detection Systems

Several different technologies are currently used to detect explosives: trace detection, quadrupole resonance analysis, and x-ray scanning machines.

Intrusion detection systems

Intrusion detection systems serve to alert security staff to react to potential security incidents. These systems are designed to identify penetrations into buildings through vulnerable perimeter barriers such as doors, windows, roofs, and walls. These systems use highly sensitive sensors that can detect an unauthorized entry or attempted entry through the phenomena of motion, vibrations, heat, or sound.

When an intrusion is sensed, a control panel to which the sensors are connected transmits a signal to a central response area, which is continually monitored by security personnel. The sensor-detected incident will alert security personnel of the incident and where it is occurring. By interfacing these technologies, security personnel can initially assess sensor-detected security events before determining how to react appropriately. See also section of close circuit television.

Intrusion Sensors

Electronic intrusion detection systems are designed to detect penetrations into secured areas through vulnerable perimeter barriers such as walls, roofs, doors, and windows. Detection is usually reported by an intrusion sensor and announced by an alarm (typically to a central response area).

Video motion detectors transform the viewing-only ability of CCTV cameras into a tracking and alarm system.

Balanced magnetic switches are an extension of the conventional magnetic switch used on doors and windows in a home security system and are widely used to indicate whether a door is open or closed.

Sonic and vibration sensors detect intrusion indicators such as the sound and movements of breaking glass or wood at windows and walls. Because they are typically used in rooms during timeframes when legitimate access is not expected, these sensors can also be used to detect the motion of a person walking into or within a designated area.

Building Structures

Critical Components

Because direct explosion effects decay rapidly with distance, the local response of structural components is the dominant concern. General principles governing the design of critical components are discussed next.

Exterior Frame

There are two primary considerations for the exterior frame. The first is to design the exterior columns to resist the direct effects of the specified threats. The second is to ensure that the exterior frame has sufficient structural integrity to accept localized failure without initiating progressive collapse.

Because columns do not have much surface area, air-blast loads on columns tend to be mitigated by "clear-time effects". This refers to the pressure wave washing around these slender tall members, and consequently the entire duration of the pressure wave does not act upon them. On the other hand, the critical threat is directly across from them, so they are loaded with the peak reflected pressure, which is typically several times larger than the incident or overpressure wave that is propagating through the air.

For columns subjected to a vehicle weapon threat on an adjacent street, buckling and shear are the primary effects to be considered in analysis. If a very large weapon is detonated close to a column, shattering of the concrete due to multiple tensile reflections within the concrete section can destroy its integrity. Buckling is a concern if lateral support is lost due to the failure of a supporting floor system. This is particularly important for buildings that are close to public streets. In this case, exterior columns should be capable of spanning two or more stories without buckling. Slender steel columns are at substantially greater risk than are concrete columns. Confinement of concrete using columns with closely spaced closed ties or spiral reinforcing will improve shear capacity, improve the performance of lap splices in the event of loss of concrete cover, and greatly enhance column ductility. The potential benefit from providing closely spaced closed ties in exterior concrete columns is very high relative to the cost of the added reinforcement.

For steel columns, splices should be placed as far above grade level as practical. It is recommended that splices at exterior columns that are not specifically designed to resist air-blast loads employ complete-penetration welded flanges. Welding details, materials, and procedures should be selected to ensure toughness.

For a package weapon, column breach is a major consideration. Some suggestions for mitigating this concern are listed below.

Do not use exposed columns that are fully or partially accessible from the building exterior. Arcade columns should be avoided.

Use an architectural covering that is at least six inches from the structural member. This will make it considerably more difficult to place a weapon directly against the structure. Because explosive pressures decay so rapidly, every inch of distance will help to protect the column.

Load- bearing reinforced concrete wall construction can provide a considerable level of protection if adequate reinforcement is provided to achieve ductile behavior. This may be an appropriate solution for the parts of the building that are closest to the secured perimeter line (within twenty feet). Masonry is a much more brittle material that is capable of generating highly hazardous flying debris in the event of an explosion. Its use is generally discouraged for new construction. Spandrel beams of limited depth generally do well when subjected to air blast. In general, edge beams are very strongly encouraged at the perimeter of concrete slab construction to afford frame action for redistribution of vertical loads and to enhance the shear connection of floors to columns.

Roof System

The primary loading on the roof is the downward air-blast pressure. The exterior bay roof system on the side(s) facing an exterior threat is the most critical. The air-blast pressure on the interior bays is less intense, so the roof there may require less hardening. Secondary loads include upward pressure due to the air blast penetrating through openings and upward suction during the negative loading phase. The upward pressure may have an increased duration due to multiple reflections of the internal air-blast wave. It is conservative to consider the downward and upward loads separately.

The preferred system is cast-in-place reinforced concrete with beams in two directions. If this system is used, beams should have continuous top and bottom reinforcement with tension lap splices. Stirrups to develop the bending capacity of the beams closely spaced along the entire span are recommended.

Somewhat lower levels of protection are afforded by conventional steel beam construction with a steel deck and concrete fill slab. The performance of this system can be enhanced by use of normal-weight concrete fill instead of lightweight fill, increasing the gauge of welded wire fabric reinforcement, and making the connection between the slab and beams with shear connector studs. Since it is anticipated that the slab capacity will exceed that of the supporting beams, beam end connections should be capable of developing the ultimate flexural capacity of the beams to avoid brittle failure. Beam-to-column connections should be capable of resisting upward as well as downward forces.

Precast and pre-/post-tensioned systems are generally considered less desirable, unless members and connections are capable of resisting upward forces generated by rebound from the direct pressure and/or the suction from the negative pressure phase of the air blast.

Concrete flat slab/plate systems are also less desirable because of the potential of shear failure at the columns. When flat slab/plate systems are used, they should include features to enhance their punching shear resistance. Continuous bottom reinforcement should be provided through columns in two directions to retain the slab in the event that punching shear failure occurs. Edge beams should be provided at the building exterior.

Lightweight systems, such as untopped steel deck or wood frame construction, are considered to afford minimal resistance to air-blast. These systems are prone to failure due to their low capacity for downward and uplift pressures.

Floor System

Remember

The floor system design should consider three possible scenarios: airblast loading, redistributing load in the event of loss of a column or wall support below, and the ability to arrest debris falling from the floor or roof above.

For structures in which the interior is secured against bombs of moderate size by package inspection, the primary concern is the exterior bay framing. For buildings that are separated from a public street only by a sidewalk, the uplift pressures from a vehicle weapon may be significant enough to cause possible failure of the exterior bay floors for several levels above ground. Special concern exists in the case of vertical irregularities in the architectural system, either where the exterior wall is set back from the floor above or where the structure steps back to form terraces.

Tips

Structural hardening of floor systems above unsecured areas of the building such as lobbies, loading docks , garages, mailrooms, and retail spaces should be considered. In general, critical or heavily occupied areas should not be placed underneath unsecured areas, since it is virtually impossible to prevent against localized breach in conventional construction for package weapons placed on the floor. Precast panels are problematic because of their tendency to fail at the connections. Pre-/post-tensioned systems tend to fail in a brittle manner if stressed much beyond their elastic limit. These systems are also not able to accept upward loads without additional reinforcement. If pre-/post-tensioned systems are used, continuous mild steel needs to be added to the top and the bottom faces to provide the ductility needed to resist explosion loads.

Flat slab/plate systems are also less desirable because of limited two way action and the potential for shear failure at the columns. When flat slab/plate systems are employed, they should include features to enhance their punching shear resistance, and continuous bottom reinforcement should be provided across columns to resist progressive collapse. Edge beams should be provided at the building exterior.

Interior Columns

Interior columns in unsecured areas are subject to many of the same issues as exterior columns. If possible, columns should not be accessible within these areas. If they are accessible, then obscure their location or impose a standoff to the structural component through the use of cladding.

Methods of hardening columns include using closely spaced ties, spiral reinforcement, and architectural covering at least six inches from the structural elements. Composite steel and concrete sections or steel plating of concrete columns can provide higher levels of protection. Columns in unsecured areas should be designed to span two or three stories without buckling in the event that the floor below and possibly above the detonation area have failed, as previously discussed.

Interior Walls

Interior walls surrounding unsecured spaces are designed to contain the explosive effects within the unsecured areas. Ideally, unsecured areas are located adjacent to the building exterior so that the explosive pressure may be vented outward as well.

Fully grouted CMU (concrete masonry unit) block walls that are well reinforced vertically and horizontally and adequately supported laterally are a common solution. Anchorage at the top and bottom of walls should be capable of developing the full flexural capacity of the wall.

Lateral support at the top of the walls may be achieved using steel angles anchored into the floor system above. Care should be taken to terminate bars at the top of the wall with hooks or heads and to ensure that the upper course of block is filled solid with grout. The base of the wall may be anchored by reinforcing bar dowels.

Interior walls can also be effective in resisting progressive collapse if they are designed properly with sufficient load-bearing capacity and are tied into the floor systems below and above.

This design for hardened interior wall construction is also recommended for primary egress routes to protect against explosions, fire, and other hazards trapping occupants.

Building Information Modeling (BIM)

BIM can be used to demonstrate the entire building life cycle, including the processes of construction and facility operation. It covers geometry, spatial relationships, light analysis, geographic information, quantities and properties of building components.

The great advantage of BIM is that it be used in the planning stage to provide rapid answers to 'what-if' scenarios. Thanks to the lightning speed of modern computers and very sophisticated software these answers can often be delivered in hours so avoiding costly building mistakes and making structures much more secure.

An advanced form of BIM is the Finite Element Method (FEM) which allows structural engineers to use simulations to identify structural weaknesses for instance, how would the structure withstand a truck bomb, a 120 mph hurricane or if it had a flat roof, two feet of standing water following days of torrential rain. A downside to FEM was that in simulated models components bent but did not separate so although you could see what would happen you did not get a complete picture of the total event.

The Applied Element Method (AEM) provides that solution. Coupled with Extreme Loading for Structures (ELS) software, engineers and architects can watch and analyze the results of progressive collapse, seismic wave effect, high wind, glass and blast. Engineers can look at every structural element exposed to the load and see first hand its predictable behavior. For example, engineers and architects can choose to change a column's design to withstand different blast loads significantly mitigating the risk of collapse.

Using AEM modeling, we now know that if the steel reinforcing bars in the main concrete girder had been doubled, the structure would have better withstood the blast and many more people would have survived.

Knowing potential vulnerabilities of a design allows the making of more informed decisions on structural design and architectural layouts, determining building envelopes and perimeters, opting for alternate material selections, and even developing better security and safety procedures.

There are also several modeling programs that can be used which for instance, allow designers to visualize the fields of view of close circuit television and areas of coverage. These programs include Google Earth, Revit SD and Sketch Up.

Structural

☐ Incorporate measures to prevent progressive collapse.

☐ Design floor systems for uplift in unsecured areas and in exterior bays that may pose a hazard to occupants.

☐ Limit column spacing.

☐ Avoid transfer girders.

☐ Use two-way floor and roof systems.

☐ Use fully grouted, heavily reinforced CMU block walls that are properly anchored in order to separate unsecured areas from critical functions and occupied secured areas.

☐ Use dynamic nonlinear analysis methods for design of critical structural components.

Note: The purpose of integrated physical security is to ensure that at the end of the day the architectural aesthetics of the buildings have been preserved while all practical security-hardening measures have been incorporated. This is even more so if the buildings have historic merit – as many federal buildings do – because of rigid codes governing what can and cannot be done.

Exterior Wall/Cladding Design

The exterior walls provide the first line of defense against the intrusion of the air-blast pressure and hazardous debris into the building. They are subject to direct reflected pressures from an explosive threat located directly across from the wall along the secured perimeter line. If the building is more than four stories high, it may be advantageous to consider the reduction in pressure with height due to the increased distance and angle of incidence. The objective of design at a minimum is to ensure that these members fail in a ductile mode such as flexure rather than a brittle mode such as shear. The walls also need to be able to resist the loads transmitted by the windows and doors. It is not uncommon, for instance, for bullet-resistant windows to have a higher ultimate capacity than the walls to which they are attached. Beyond ensuring a ductile failure mode, the exterior wall may be designed to resist the actual or reduced pressure levels of the defined threat. Note that special reinforcing and anchors should be provided around blast resistant window and door frames.

Poured-in-place, reinforced concrete will provide the highest level of protection, but solutions like pre-cast concrete, CMU block, and metal stud systems may also be used to achieve lower levels of protection.

For pre-cast panels, consider a minimum thickness of five inches exclusive of reveals, with two-way, closely spaced reinforcing bars to increase ductility and reduce the chance of flying concrete fragments. The objective is to reduce the loads transmitted into the connections, which need to be designed to resist the ultimate flexural resistance of the panels.

Also, connections into the structure should provide as straight a line of load transmittal as practical.

For CMU block walls, use eight-inch block walls, fully grouted with vertically centered heavy reinforcing bars and horizontal reinforcement placed at each layer. Connections into the structure should be designed to resist the ultimate lateral capacity of the wall. For infill walls, avoid transferring loads into the columns if they are primary load-carrying elements.

The connection details may be very difficult to construct. It will be difficult to have all the blocks fit over the bars near the top, and it will be difficult to provide the required lateral restraint at the top connection.

A preferred system is to have a continuous exterior CMU wall that laterally bears against the floor system. For increased protection, consider using 12-inch blocks with two layers of vertical reinforcement.

For metal stud systems, use metal studs back-to-back and mechanically attached, to minimize lateral torsional effects. To catch exterior cladding fragments, attach a wire mesh or steel sheet to the exterior side of the metal stud system. The supports of the wall should be designed to resist the ultimate lateral out-of-plane bending capacity load of the system.

Brick veneers and other nonstructural elements attached to the building exterior are to be avoided or have strengthened connections to limit flying debris and to improve emergency egress by ensuring that exits remain passable.

Window Design

Remember Windows, once the sole responsibility of the architect, become a structural issue when explosive effects are taken into consideration. In designing windows to mitigate the effects of explosions they should first be designed to resist conventional loads and then be checked for explosive load effects and balanced design.

Balanced or capacity design philosophy means that the glass is designed to be no stronger than the weakest part of the overall window system, failing at pressure levels that do not exceed those of the frame, anchorage, and supporting wall system. If the glass is stronger than the supporting members, then the window is likely to fail with the whole panel entering into the building as a single unit, possibly with the frame, anchorage, and the wall attached. This failure mode is considered more hazardous than if the glass fragments enter the building, provided that the fragments are designed to minimize injuries. By using a damage-limiting approach, the damage sequence and extent of damage can be controlled.

Remember Windows are typically the most vulnerable portion of any building.

Though it may be impractical to design all the windows to resist a large scale explosive attack, it is desirable to limit the amount of hazardous glass breakage to reduce the injuries. Typical annealed glass windows break at low pressure and impulse levels and the shards created by broken windows are responsible for many of the injuries incurred during a large-scale explosive attack.

Designing windows to provide protection against the effects of explosions can be effective in reducing the glass laceration injuries in areas that are not directly across from the weapon. For a large-scale vehicle weapon, this pressure range is expected on the sides of surrounding buildings not facing the explosion or for smaller explosions in which pressures drop more rapidly with distance. Generally, it is not known on which side of the building the attack will occur, so all sides need to be protected. Window protection should be evaluated on a case-by-case basis by a qualified protective design consultant to develop a solution that meets established objectives.

Several approaches can be taken to limit glass laceration injuries. One way is to reduce the number and size of windows. If blast-resistant walls are used, then fewer and/or smaller windows will allow less air blast to enter the building, thus reducing the interior damage and injuries.

Specific examples of how to incorporate these ideas into the design of a new building include (1) limiting the number of windows on the lower floors where the pressures would be higher during an external explosion; (2) using an internal atrium design with windows facing inward, not outward; (3) using clerestory windows, which are close to the ceiling, above the heads of the occupants; and (4) angling the windows away from the curb to reduce the pressure levels.

Glass curtain-wall, butt glazed, and Pilkington type systems have been found to perform surprisingly well in recent explosive tests with low explosive loads. In particular, glass curtain wall systems have been shown to accept larger deformations without the glass breaking hazardously, compared to rigidly supported punched window systems. Some design modifications to the connections, details, and member sizes may be required to optimize the performance.

Retrofitting Windows. One of the most common means of decreasing the hazards from broken glass is to install fragment-retention film on the glass. The film is a plastic (polyester) sheet that adheres to the window glass with a special adhesive. The film does not strengthen the glass; but when the glass breaks, it keeps the fragments from spreading throughout the room. The glass fragments stick to the film, and the film either stays in the window frame or falls into the room in one or more large, relatively non-hazardous pieces instead of many small, lethal pieces. Another retrofit approach is to install a blast curtain or a heavy drape behind the window. The curtain or drape catches the glass fragments. The curtains are generally used with fragment-retention film. Another retrofit technique is to use fragment retention film with a metal bar placed across the window. This "catcher bar" catches the window. The designs for this and other types of retrofit devices are complicated and require specialized engineering-analysis tools. The retrofit techniques are generally thought of as providing a lower level of protection than the glazing replacement techniques.

Glass Design

Glass is often the weakest part of a building, breaking at low pressures compared to other components such as the floors, walls, or columns.

Remember

Past incidents have shown that glass breakage and associated injuries may extend many thousands of feet in large external explosions. High velocity glass fragments have been shown to be a major contributor to injuries in such incidents. For incidents within downtown city areas, falling glass poses a major hazard to passersby and prolongs post-incident rescue and clean-up efforts by leaving tons of glass debris on the street. As part of the damage-limiting approach, glass failure is not quantified in terms of whether breakage occurs or not, but rather by the hazard it causes to the occupants. Two failure modes that reduce the hazard posed by window glass are glass that breaks but is retained by the frame and glass fragments exit the frame and fall within three to ten feet of the window.

The glass performance conditions are defined based on empirical data from explosive tests performed in a cubical space with a 10- foot dimension. The performance condition ranges from 1, which corresponds to not breaking, to 5, which corresponds to hazardous flying debris at a distance of 10 feet from the window. Generally a performance condition 3 or 4 is considered acceptable for buildings that are not at high risk of attack. At this level, the window breaks and fragments fly into the building but land harmlessly within 10 feet of the window or impact a witness panel 10 feet away, no more than 2 feet above the floor level. The design goal is to achieve a performance level less than 4 for 90 percent of the windows.

The preferred solution for new construction is to use laminated annealed (i.e., float) glass with structural sealant around the inside perimeter. For insulated units, only the inner pane needs to be laminated. The lamination holds the shards of glass together in explosive events, reducing its ability to cause laceration injuries. The structural sealant helps to hold the pane in the frame for higher loads. Annealed glass is used because it has a breaking strength that is about one-half that of heat-strengthened glass and about one-fourth as strong as tempered glass. Using annealed glass becomes particularly important for buildings with lightweight exterior walls using for instance, metal studs, dry wall, and brick façade. Use the thinnest overall glass thickness that is acceptable based on conventional load requirements. Also, it is important to use an interlayer thickness that is 60 mil thick rather than 30 mil thick, as is used in conventional applications. This layup has been shown to perform well in low-pressure regions (i.e., under about 5 psi).

If a 60 mil polyvinyl butaryl (PVB) layer is used, the tension membrane forces into the framing members need to be considered in design.

To make sure that the components supporting the glass are stronger than the glass itself, specify a window breakage strength that is high compared to what is used in conventional design. The breakage strength in window design may be specified as a function of the number of windows expected to break at that load. For instance, in conventional design, it is typical to use a breakage pressure corresponding to eight breaks out of 1000. When a lot of glass breakage is expected, such as for an explosive incident, use a pressure corresponding to 750 breaks out of 1000 to increase confidence that the frame does not fail, too. Glass breakage strength values may be obtained from window manufacturers.

Mullion Design

The frame members connecting adjoining windows are referred to as mullions. These members may be designed in two ways. Using a static approach, the breaking strength of the window glass is applied to the mullion; alternatively, a dynamic load can be applied using the peak pressure and impulse values. The static approach may lead to a design that is not practical, because the mullion can become very deep and heavy, driving up the weight and cost of the window system. It may also not be consistent with the overall architectural objectives for the project.

As with frames, it is good engineering practice to limit the number of interlocking parts used for the mullion.

Frame and Anchorage Design

Window frames need to retain the glass so that the entire pane does not become a single large unit of flying debris. It also needs to be designed to resist the breaking stress of the window glass.

To retain the glass in the frame, a minimum of a ¼-inch bead of structural sealant (e.g., silicone) should be used around the inner perimeter of the window. The allowable tensile strength should be at least 20 psi.

Also, the window bite (i.e., the depth of window captured by the frame) needs to be at least ½ inch. The structural sealant recommendations should be determined on a case-by-case basis. In some applications, the structural sealant may govern the overall design of the window system.

Frame and anchorage design is performed by applying the breaking strength of the window to the frame and the fasteners. In most conventionally designed buildings, the frames will be aluminum. In some applications, steel frames are used. Also, in lobby areas where large panes of glass are used, a larger bite with more structural sealant may be needed.

Inoperable windows are generally recommended for air-blast mitigating designs. However, some operable window designs are conceptually viable.

For instance, designs in which the window rotates about a horizontal hinge at the head or sill and opens in the outward direction may perform adequately. In these designs, the window will slam shut in an explosion event. If this type of design is used, the governing design parameter may be the capacity of the hinges and/or hardware.

Wall Design

The supporting wall response should be checked using approaches similar to those for frames and mullions. It does not make sense, and is potentially highly hazardous, to have a wall system that is weaker than windows. Remember that the maximum strength of any wall system needs to be at least equal to the window strength. If the walls are unable to accept the loads transmitted by the mullions, the mullions may need to be anchored into the structural slabs or spandrel beams. Anchoring into columns is generally discouraged, because it increases the tributary area of lateral load that is transferred into the columns and may cause instability.

The balanced-design approach is particularly challenging in the design of ballistic-resistant and forced-entry-resistant windows, which consist of one or more inches of glass and polycarbonate. These windows can easily become stronger than the supporting wall. In these cases, the windows may need to be designed for the design threat air-blast pressure levels under the implicit assumption that balanced-design conditions will not be met for larger loads.

Multi-hazard Considerations

Under normal operating conditions, windows perform several functions listed below.

☐ They permit light to enter building.

☐ They save energy by reducing thermal transmission.

☐ They make the building quieter by reducing acoustic transmission.

Explosions are one of a number of abnormal loading conditions that the building may undergo. Some of the others are:

☐ Fire

☐ Earthquake

☐ Hurricane

☐ gun fire, and

☐ forced entry.

When developing a protection strategy for windows to mitigate the effects of a particular explosion threat scenario, it is important to consider how this protection may interfere with some of these other functions or other explosion threat scenarios. Some questions that may be worthwhile to consider are listed below.

☐ If an internal explosion occurs, will the upgraded windows increase smoke inhalation injuries by preventing the smoke to vent through windows that would normally break in an explosion event?

☐ If a fire occurs, will it be more difficult to break the protected windows to vent the building and gain access to the injured?

☐ Will a window upgrade that is intended to protect the occupants worsen the hazard to passersby?

Other Openings

Doors, louvers, and other openings in the exterior envelope should be designed so that the anchorage into the supporting structure has a lateral capacity greater than that of the element.

There are two general recommendations for doors.

☐ Doors should open outward so that they bear against the jamb during the positive-pressure phase of the air-blast loading.

☐ Door jambs can be filled with concrete to improve their resistance.

For louvers that provide air to sensitive equipment, some recommendations are given below.

☐ Provide a baffle in front of the louver so that the air blast does not have direct line-of-sight access through the louver.

☐ Provide a grid of steel bars properly anchored into the structure behind the louver to catch any debris generated by the louver or other flying fragments.

Building Envelope

Cladding

Use the thinnest panel thickness that is acceptable for conventional loads.

Design cladding supports and the supporting structure to resist the ultimate lateral resistance of the panel.

Design cladding connections to have as direct a load transmission path into the main structure as practical. A good transmission path minimizes shear and torsional response.

Avoid framing cladding into columns and other primary vertical load-carrying members. Instead frame into floor diaphragms.

Windows

Use the thinnest glass section that is acceptable for conventional loads.

Design window systems so that the frame anchorage and the supporting wall are capable of resisting the breaking pressure of the window glass.

Use laminated annealed glass (for insulated panels, only the interior pane needs to be laminated).

Design window frames with a minimum of a ½-inch bite.

Use a minimum of a ¼-inch silicone sealant around the inside glass perimeter, with a minimum tensile strength of 20 psi.

Mechanical And Electrical Systems

In the event of an explosion directed at a high-occupancy building, the primary objective is to protect people by preventing building collapse. Secondary goals are to limit injuries due to flying building debris and the direct effects of air blast entering the building (i.e., impact due to being thrown or lung collapse). Beyond these life-safety concerns, the objective is to facilitate building evacuation and rescue efforts through effective building design.

Must Do

The key concepts for providing secure and effective mechanical and electrical systems in buildings is the same as for the other building systems: separation, hardening, and redundancy. Keeping critical mechanical and electrical functions as far from high-threat areas as possible (e.g., lobbies, loading docks, mail rooms, garages, and retail spaces) increases their ability to survive an event. Separation is perhaps the most cost-effective option. Additionally, physical hardening or protection of these systems (including the conduits, pipes, and ducts associated with life-safety systems) provides increased likelihood that they will be able to survive the direct effects of the event if they are close enough to be affected. Finally, by providing redundant emergency systems that are adequately separated, there is a greater likelihood that emergency systems will remain operational post-event to assist rescuers in the evacuation of the building.

Architecturally, enhancements to mechanical and electrical systems will require additional space to accommodate additional equipment. Fortunately, there are many incremental improvements that can be made that require only a small change to the design. Additional space can be provided for future enhancements as funds or the risk justify implementation.

Structurally, the walls and floor systems adjacent to the areas where critical equipment are located need to be protected by means of hardening.

Other areas where hardening is recommended include primary egress routes, feeders for emergency power distribution, sprinkler systems mains and risers, fire alarm system trunk wiring, and ducts used for smoke-control systems.

From an operational security standpoint, it is important to restrict and control access to air-intake louvers, mechanical and electrical rooms, telecommunications spaces and rooftops by means of such measures as visitor screening, limited elevator stops, close-circuit television (CCTV), detection, and card access-control systems.

Specific recommendations are given below for (1) emergency egress routes, (2) the emergency power system, (3) fuel storage, (4) transformers, (5) ventilation systems, (6) the fire control center, (7) emergency elevators, (8) the smoke and fire detection and alarm system, (9) the sprinkler/standpipe system, (10) smoke control system, and (11) the communication system.

Emergency Egress Routes

To facilitate evacuation consider these measures.

☐ Provide positive pressurization of stairwells and vestibules.

☐ Provide battery packs for lighting fixtures and exit signs.

☐ Harden walls using reinforced CMU block properly anchored at supports.

☐ Use non-slip phosphorescent treads.

☐ Do not cluster egress routes in single shaft. Separate them as far as possible.

☐ Use double doors for mass evacuation.

☐ Do not use glass along primary egress routes or stairwells.

Emergency Power System

An emergency generator provides an alternate source of power should utility power become unavailable to critical life-safety systems such as alarm systems, egress lighting fixtures, exit signs, emergency communications systems, smoke-control equipment, and fire pumps.

Tips

Emergency generators typically require large louvers to allow for ventilation of the generator while running. Care should be taken to locate the generator so that these louvers are not vulnerable to attack. A remote radiator system could be used to reduce the louver size.

Redundant emergency generator systems remotely located from each other enable the supply of emergency power from either of two locations.

Consider locating emergency power-distribution feeders in hardened enclosures, or encased in concrete , and configured in redundant routing paths to enhance reliability. Emergency distribution panels and automatic transfer switches should be located in rooms separate from the normal power system (hardened rooms, where possible).

Tips

Emergency lighting fixtures and exit signs along the egress path could be provided with integral battery packs, which locates the power source directly at the load, to provide lighting instantly in the event of a utility power outage.

It is also important to protect data communications and communications – both hardening and building in redundancy.

Fuel Storage

A non-explosive fuel source, such as diesel fuel, is acceptable for standby use for emergency generators and diesel fire pumps. Fuel tanks should be located away from building access points, in fire-rated, hardened enclosures. Fuel piping within the building should be located in hardened enclosures, and redundant piping systems could be provided to enhance the reliability of the fuel distribution system. Fuel filling stations should be located away from public access points and monitored by the CCTV system.

Tips

Transformers

Main power transformer(s) should be located interior to the building if possible, away from locations accessible to the public. For larger buildings, multiple transformers, located remotely from each other, could enhance reliability should one transformer be damaged by an explosion.

Ventilation Systems

Air-intake locations should be located as high up in the building as is practical to limit access to the general public. Systems that serve public access areas such as mail receiving rooms, loading docks, lobbies, freight elevators/lobbies should be isolated and provided with dedicated air handling systems capable of 100 percent exhaust mode. Tie air intake locations and fan rooms into the security surveillance and alarm system.

Building HVAC systems are typically controlled by a building automation system, which allows for quick response to shut down or selectively control air conditioning systems. This system is coordinated with the smoke-control and fire-alarm systems.

Fire Control Center

A Fire Control Center should be provided to monitor alarms and life safety components, operate smoke-control systems, communicate with occupants, and control the fire-fighting/evacuation process. Consider providing redundant Fire Control Centers remotely located from each other to allow system operation and control from alternate locations. The Fire Control Center should be located near the point of firefighter access to the building. If the control center is adjacent to lobby, separate it from the lobby using a corridor or other buffer area. Provide hardened construction for the Fire Control Center.

Emergency Elevators

Elevators are not used as a means of egress from a building in the event of a life-safety emergency event, as conventional elevators are not suitably protected from the penetration of smoke into the elevator shaft.

An unwitting passenger could be endangered if an elevator door opens onto a smoke filled lobby. Firefighters may elect to manually use an elevator for firefighting or rescue operation.

A dedicated elevator, within its own hardened, smoke-proof enclosure, could enhance the firefighting and rescue operation after a blast/fire event. The dedicated elevator should be supplied from the emergency generator, fed by conduit/wire that is protected in hardened enclosures. This shaft/lobby assembly should be sealed and positively pressurized to prevent the penetration of smoke into the protected area.

Smoke and Fire Detection and Alarm System

A combination of early-warning smoke detectors, sprinkler-flow switches, manual pull stations, and audible and visual alarms provide quick response and notification of an event. The activation of any device will automatically start the sequence of operation of smoke control, egress, and communication systems to allow occupants to quickly go to a safe area. System designs should include redundancy such as looped infrastructure wiring and distributed intelligence such that the severing of the loop will not disable the system. Install a fire-alarm system consisting of distributed intelligent fire alarm panels connected in a peer-to-peer network, such that each panel can function independently and process alarms and initiate sequences within its respective zone.

Sprinkler/Standpipe System

Sprinklers will automatically suppress fire in the area upon sensing heat. Sprinkler activation will activate the fire alarm system. Standpipes have water available locally in large quantities for use by professional fire fighters. Multiple sprinkler and standpipe risers limit the possibility of an event severing all water supply available to fight a fire.

Redundant water services would increase the reliability of the source for sprinkler protection and fire suppression. Appropriate valving should be provided where services are combined.

Redundant fire pumps could be provided in remote locations. These pumps could rely on different sources, for example one electric pump supplied from the utility and/or emergency generator and a second diesel fuel source fire pump.

Diverse and separate routing of standpipe and sprinkler risers within hardened areas will enhance the system's reliability (i.e., reinforced masonry walls at stair shafts containing standpipes).

Smoke-Control Systems

Appropriate smoke-control systems maintain smoke-free paths of egress for building occupants through a series of fans, ductwork, and fire smoke dampers. Stair pressurization systems maintain a clear path of egress for occupants to safe areas or to evacuate the building. Smoke control fans should be located higher in a building rather than at lower floors to limit exposure/access to external vents. Vestibules at stairways with separate pressurization provide an additional layer of smoke control.

Communication System

A voice communication system facilitates the orderly control of occupants and evacuation of the danger area or the entire building. The system is typically zoned by floor, by stairwell, and by elevator bank for selective communication to building occupants.

Remember

Emergency communication can be enhanced by providing

☐ extra emergency phones separate from the telephone system, connected directly to a constantly supervised central station;

☐ in-building repeater system for police, fire, and EMS (Emergency Medical Services) radios; and

☐ redundant or wireless fireman's communications in building.

Mechanical and Electrical Systems

☐ Place all emergency functions away from high-risk areas in protected locations with restricted access.

☐ Provide redundant and separated emergency functions.

☐ Harden and/or provide physical buffer zones for the enclosures around emergency equipment, controls, and wiring.

☐ For egress routes, provide battery packs for exit signs, use non-slip phosphorescent treads, and double doors for mass evacuation.

☐ Avoid using glass along primary egress routes or stairwells.

☐ Place emergency functions away from structurally vulnerable areas such as transfer girders.

☐ Place a transformer interior to building, if possible.

☐ Provide access to the fire control center from the building exterior.

Design

Site design and planning

Remember

The single most important goal in planning a site or retrofitting one to resist terrorism and security threats is the protection of life, property, and operations. Decision-making in support of this purpose should be based first and foremost on a comprehensive assessment of the manmade threats and hazards so that planning and design countermeasures are appropriate and effective in the reduction of vulnerability and risk. It is important to recognize that a given countermeasure can mitigate one or more vulnerabilities, but may be detrimental to other important design goals. It is also important to think creatively and comprehensively about the security repercussions of common site planning and design decisions. This section will highlight several aspects of site design and will present some of the unique characteristics arising from their application to antiterrorism and security.

Site Design

Remember

Because the economics of development dictate recovering the largest possible portion of square footage within most urban and rural sites, security concerns should be evaluated carefully. Conflicts sometimes arise between security site design and conventional site design. For example, open circulation and common spaces, which are desirable for conventional design, are often undesirable for security design. To maximize safety, security, and sustainability, designers should implement a holistic approach to site design that integrates form and function to achieve a balance among the various design elements and objectives. Even if resources are limited, significant value can be added to a project by integrating security considerations into the more traditional design tasks in such a way that they complement, rather than compete with, the other elements.

Layout and Form

The overall layout of a site (e.g., the placement and form of its buildings, infrastructures, and amenities) is the starting point for development. Choices made during this stage of the design process will steer decision-making for the other elements of the site. A number of aspects of site layout and building type present security considerations and are discussed below.

Building Placement

Depending on the site characteristics, the occupancy requirements, and other factors, buildings may be clustered tightly in one area, or dispersed across the site. Both patterns have compelling strengths and weaknesses. Concentrating people, property, and operations in one place creates a target-rich environment, and the mere proximity of any one building to any other may increase the risk of collateral impacts. Additionally, the potential exists for the establishment of more single-point vulnerabilities in a clustered design than would exist in a more dispersed pattern. However, grouping high-risk activities, concentrations of personnel, and critical functions into a cluster can help maximize stand-off from the perimeter and create a "defensible space." This also helps to reduce the number of access and surveillance points, and minimize the size of the perimeter needed to protect the facilities. In addition, combining multiple uses also provides economic and environmental benefits such as opportunities to efficiently transfer heat from net heat-producing areas and activities to net heat-consuming ones, thus reducing energy costs. In contrast, the dispersal of buildings, people, and operations across the site reduces the risk that an attack on any one part of the site will impact the other parts. However, this could also have an isolating effect, and reduce the effectiveness of on-site surveillance, increase the complexity of security systems and emergency response, and create a less defensible space.

To the extent that site, economics, and other factors allow, the designer should consolidate buildings that are functionally compatible and have similar threat levels. For example, visitor screening areas, receiving/loading areas, and mailrooms constitute the innermost line of defense, because they may be the first places where people and materials are closely inspected before being introduced into the facility. Logically, they should be physically separated from the key assets such as main operational areas and concentrations of people. It is also desirable to locate potential target buildings away from lower-risk areas in order to minimize collateral damage, should an attack occur.

Remember

Building Orientation

The orientation of a building can have significant impact on its performance, not only in terms of energy efficiency, but also in the ability to protect occupants. For the purposes of this discussion, the term "orientation" refers to three distinct characteristics: the building's spatial relationship to the site, its orientation relative to the sun, and its vertical or horizontal aspect relative to the ground.

A structure's orientation relative to its surroundings defines its relationship to that area. In aesthetic terms, a building can "open up" to the area or turn its back; it can be inviting to those outside, or it can "hunker down" defensively. The physical positioning of a building relative to its surroundings may seem subtle, but can be a greater determinant of this intangible quality than exterior aesthetics.

Remember

Nevertheless, the proximity of a vulnerable facade to a parking area, street, adjacent site, or other area that is accessible to vehicles and/or difficult to observe can greatly contribute to its vulnerability. This illustrates one way in which protective requirements can be at odds with otherwise good design. A strong, blank wall with no glazing will help to protect the people, property, and operations within from a blast, but the lack of windows removes virtually all opportunity to monitor activities outside and take appropriate protective actions in a timely manner. Designers should consider such trade-offs early in the design process, in an effort to determine an acceptable level of risk.

The solar orientation of a building is a significant factor in energy consumption. By optimizing the positioning of the building relative to the sun, climate control and lighting requirements can be met while reducing power consumption. However, these energy conservation techniques present some important security considerations. For example, natural ventilation is an effective and time-tested technique for efficiently cooling buildings; however, the use of unfiltered outside air presents a major vulnerability to aerosolized chemical, biological, and radiological agents, in addition to accidental releases of hazardous materials.

Additionally, awnings may become projectiles in a blast event, and the construction of operable windows may not be as blast-resistant as the frames of fixed windows. Similarly, the use of light shelves, skylights, clerestories, and atria can help meet illumination requirements while dramatically reducing the need for electric lighting. However, day lighting relies inherently on the use of glazing, which has been shown to be one of the major hazards in blast events. In addition to ensuring the maximum setback possible for highly-fenestrated facades, designers should ensure that aperture sizes, glazing materials, films, and frames and connections are selected with blast-resistance as well as energy efficiency in mind.

Open space

The incorporation of open space into site design presents a number of benefits. First and foremost is the ability to easily monitor an area and detect intruders, vehicles, and weapons. Closely related to this benefit is the stand-off value of open space; blast energy decreases as the inverse of the cube of the distance from the seat of the explosion, so every additional increment of distance provides increasingly more protection. In addition, pervious open space allows stormwater to percolate back into the ground, reducing the need for culverts, drainage pipes, manholes, and other covert site access and weapon concealment opportunities. Also, if the open space is impassible for vehicles (as in the case of a wetland or densely vegetated area), it can provide not only environmental and aesthetic amenities, but prevent vehicle intrusion as well. Leaving significant amounts of open space, wetland, or other sensitive areas unimproved may present opportunities to reap economic benefits in the form of transferable development rights (TDRs). TDR is a market-based approach that provides incentives to developers to focus growth only where it is desired, making it profitable to refrain from developing open space and sensitive areas. By not maximizing the profit potential of their land, owners can receive "development right credits" that can be sold to developers elsewhere in the community, who will then be able to use those credits to intensify the use of their own land in ways that promote more sustainable growth. Thus, in some cases, TDRs may be a windfall benefit of security-oriented development.

Some other design considerations

Designing a security project is similar to any other design project yet has several critical differences that should be pointed out:

- ☐ Confidentiality – security is essential because of the sensitive nature of the work.
- ☐ Client based core team/ owners representative
- ☐ Levels of design
- ☐ Conceptual Design
- ☐ Traditional design
- ☐ Design / Build
- ☐ Turnkey
- ☐ Design phases & milestones
- ☐ Programming
- ☐ Design - Schematic design, design development, Construction Documents
- ☐ Cost Estimate
- ☐ Permitting
- ☐ Services During Construction
- ☐ RFI's
- ☐ Submittals
- ☐ Record Drawings
- ☐ O&M's
- ☐ Facility as-builds
- ☐ System redundancy / Spare Capacity
- ☐ Design deliverables
- ☐ Phasing

☐ QA/QC

☐ Design reviews

☐ Packaging strategies

☐ Confidentiality

☐ Impacts to existing operations

☐ Communications w/ local 1st responders

☐ Balancing physical protection systems & operational procedures

☐ Emergency egress, Code compliance, ADA requirements

☐ System Integration

☐ Hazards

☐ Protecting against explosive, chemical, biological and radiological attacks.

☐ Designing security into a building requires a complex series of tradeoffs.

Security concerns need to be balanced with many other design constraints such as accessibility, initial and life-cycle costs, natural hazard mitigation, fire protection, energy efficiency, and aesthetics.

Because the probability of attack may be small, security measures should not interfere with daily operations of the building. On the other hand, because the effects of attack can be catastrophic, it is prudent to incorporate measures that may save lives and minimize business interruption in the unlikely event of an attack. The measures should be as unobtrusive as possible to provide an inviting, efficient environment that does not attract undue attention of potential attackers. Security design needs to be part of an overall multi-hazard approach to ensure that it does not worsen the behavior of the building in the event of a fire, earthquake, or hurricane, which are far more prevalent hazards than are terrorist attacks.

Because of the severity of the types of hazards discussed, the goals of security-oriented design are by necessity modest. With regard to explosive attacks, the focus is on a damage-limiting or damage-mitigating approach rather than a blast-resistant approach. The goal is to incorporate some reasonable measures that will enhance the life safety of the persons within the building and facilitate rescue efforts in the unlikely event of attack.

Protection against terrorist attack is not an all-or-nothing proposition. Incremental measures taken early in design may be more fully developed at a later date. With a little forethought regarding, for instance, the space requirements needed to accommodate additional measures, the protection level can be enhanced as the need arises or the budget permits after construction is complete.

FEMA advocates a holistic multi-disciplinary approach to security design by considering the various building systems including site, architecture, structure, mechanical and electrical systems and providing general recommendations for the design professional with little or no background in this area.

If you are designing a new building you can strategically site it as far from the perimeter as you can and secure the perimeter against vehicular intrusion using landscaping or barrier methods. Incorporating these security elements into an existing facility requires a different design approach.

Best practices recommended by FEMA for new buildings are listed below. The security concepts involved, however, and the remedies are equally applicable to existing buildings and facilities.

- ☐ Place building as far from any secured perimeter as practical.
- ☐ Secure the perimeter against vehicular intrusion using landscaping or barrier methods.
- ☐ Use lightweight nonstructural elements on the building exterior and interior.
- ☐ Place unsecured areas exterior to the main structure or in the exterior bay.
- ☐ Incorporate measures to resist progressive collapse.
- ☐ Design exterior window systems and cladding so that the framing, connections, and supporting structure have a lateral-load-resistance that is equal to or higher than the transparency or panel.
- ☐ Place air intakes as far above the ground level as practical.
- ☐ Physically isolate vulnerable areas such as the entries and delivery areas from the rest of the structure by using floor-to-floor walls in these areas.
- ☐ Use redundant, separated mechanical/electrical control systems.

Overview of Possible Threats

Explosive Threats:
- ☐ Vehicle weapon
- ☐ Hand-delivered weapon

Airborne Chemical, Biological, and Radiological Threats:
- ☐ Large-scale, external, air-borne release
- ☐ External release targeting building
- ☐ Internal release

Although it is possible that the dominant threat mode may change in the future, bombings have historically been a favorite tactic of terrorists. Ingredients for homemade bombs are easily obtained on the open market, as are the techniques for making bombs. Bombings are easy and quick to execute. Finally, the dramatic component of explosions in terms of the sheer destruction they cause creates a media sensation that is highly effective in transmitting the terrorist's message to the public.

Explosive Attacks

Remember

From the standpoint of structural design, the vehicle bomb is the most important consideration. Vehicle bombs are able to deliver a sufficiently large quantity of explosives to cause potentially devastating structural damage. Security design intended to limit or mitigate damage from a vehicle bomb assumes that the bomb is detonated at a so-called critical location. For a vehicle bomb, the critical location is taken to be at the closest point that a vehicle can approach, assuming that all security measures are in place. This may be a parking area directly beneath the occupied building, the loading dock, the curb directly outside the facility, or at a vehicle-access control gate where inspection takes place, depending on the level of protection incorporated into the design.

Another explosive attack threat is the small bomb that is hand delivered.

Small weapons can cause the greatest damage when brought into vulnerable, unsecured areas of the building interior, such as the building lobby, mail room, and retail spaces. Recent events around the world make it clear that there is an increased likelihood that bombs will be delivered by persons who are willing to sacrifice their own lives. Hand-carried explosives are typically on the order of five to ten pounds of TNT equivalent. However, larger charge weights, in the 50 to 100 pounds TNT equivalent range, can be readily carried in rolling cases. Mail bombs are typically less than ten pounds of TNT equivalent.

In general, the largest credible explosive size is a function of the security measures in place. Each line of security may be thought of as a sieve, reducing the size of the weapon that may gain access. Therefore the largest weapons are considered in totally unsecured public space (e.g., in a vehicle on the nearest public street), and the smallest weapons are considered in the most secured areas of the building (e.g., in a briefcase smuggled past the screening station).

Two parameters define the design threat: the weapon size, measured in equivalent pounds of TNT, and the standoff. The standoff is the distance measured from the center of gravity of the charge to the component of interest.

The design weapon size is usually selected by the owner in collaboration with security and protective design consultants (i.e., engineers who specialize in the design of structures to mitigate the effects of explosions). Although there are few unclassified sources giving the sizes of weapons that have been used in previous attacks throughout the world, security consultants have valuable information that may be used to evaluate the range of charge weights that might be reasonably considered for the intended occupancy. Security consultants draw upon the experience of other countries such as Great Britain and Israel where terrorist attacks have been more prevalent, as well as data gathered by U.S. sources.

To put the weapon size into perspective, it should be noted that thousands of deliberate explosions occur every year within the United States, but the vast majority of them have weapon yields less than five pounds. The number of large-scale vehicle weapon attacks that have used hundreds of pounds of TNT during the past twenty years is by comparison very small.

The design vehicle weapon size will usually be much smaller than the largest credible threat. The design weapon size is typically measured in hundreds of pounds rather than thousands of pounds of TNT equivalent.

The decision is usually based on a trade-off between the largest credible attack directed against the building and the design constraints of the project. Further, it is common for the design pressures and impulses to be less than the actual peak pressures and impulses acting on the building. This is the approach that the federal government has taken in their design criteria for federally owned domestic office buildings.

There are several reasons for this choice.

☐ The likely target is often not the building under design, but a high risk building that is nearby. Historically, more building damage has been due to collateral effects than direct attack.

☐ It is difficult to quantify the risk of man-made hazards. However, qualitatively it may be stated that the chance of a large-scale terrorist attack occurring is extremely low. A smaller explosive attack is far more likely.

☐ Providing a level of protection that is consistent with standards adopted for federal office buildings enhances opportunities for leasing to government agencies in addition to providing a clear statement regarding the building's safety to other potential tenants.

☐ The added robustness inherent in designing for a vehicle bomb of moderate size will improve the performance of the building under all explosion scenarios.

Description Of Explosion Forces

An explosion is an extremely rapid release of energy in the form of light, heat, sound, and a shock wave. The shock wave consists of highly compressed air that wave-reflects off the ground surface to produce a hemispherical propagation of the wave that travels outward from the source at supersonic velocities. As the shock wave expands, the incident or over-pressures decrease. When it encounters a surface that is in line-of-sight of the explosion, the wave is reflected, resulting in a tremendous amplification of pressure. Unlike acoustical waves, which reflect with an amplification factor of two, shock waves can reflect with an amplification factor of up to thirteen, due to the supersonic velocity of the shock wave at impact. The magnitude of the reflection factor is a function of the proximity of the explosion and the angle of incidence of the shock wave on the surface.

The pressures decay rapidly with time (i.e., exponentially), measured typically in thousandths of a second (milliseconds). Diffraction effects, caused by building features such as re-entrant corners and overhangs of the building may act to confine the air blast, prolonging its duration.

Late in the explosive event, the shock wave becomes negative, followed by a partial vacuum, which creates suction behind the shock wave. Immediately following the vacuum, air rushes in, creating a powerful wind or drag pressure on all surfaces of the building. This wind picks up and carries flying debris in the vicinity of the detonation.

In an external explosion, a portion of the energy is also imparted to the ground, creating a crater and generating a ground shock wave analogous to a high-intensity, short-duration earthquake. The peak pressure is a function of the weapon size or yield, and the cube of the distance.

The extent and severity of damage and injuries in an explosive event cannot be predicted with perfect certainty. For instance, two adjacent columns of a building may be roughly the same distance from the explosion, but only one fails because it is struck by a fragment in a particular way that initiates collapse. The other, by chance, is not struck and remains in place. Similarly, glass failures may occur outside of the predicted areas due to air-blast diffraction effects caused by the arrangement of buildings and their heights in the vicinity of the explosion. The details of the physical setting surrounding a particular occupant may greatly influence the level of injury incurred. The position of the person, seated or standing, facing towards or away from the event as it happens, may result in injuries ranging from minor to severe.

Despite these uncertainties, it is possible to calculate the expected extent of damage and injuries in an explosive event, based on the size of the explosion, distance from the event, and assumptions about the construction of the building. Additionally, there is strong evidence to support a relationship between injury patterns and structural damage patterns.

Damage due to the air-blast shock wave may be divided into direct airblast effects and progressive collapse. Direct air-blast effects are damage caused by the high-intensity pressures of the air blast close to the explosion. These may induce localized failure of exterior walls, windows, roof systems, floor systems, and columns.

Progressive collapse refers to the spread of an initial local failure from element to element, eventually resulting in a disproportionate extent of collapse relative to the zone of initial damage. Localized damage due to direct air-blast effects may or may not progress, depending on the design and construction of the building. To produce a progressive collapse, the weapon must be in close proximity to a critical load-bearing element. Progressive collapse can propagate vertically upward or downward from the source of the explosion, and it can propagate laterally from bay to bay as well.

The pressures that an explosion exerts on building surfaces may be several orders of magnitude greater than the loads for which the building is designed. The shock wave also acts in directions that the building may not have been designed for, such as upward pressure on the floor system.

In terms of sequence of response, the air blast first impinges the exterior envelope of the building. The pressure wave pushes on the exterior walls and may cause wall failure and window breakage. As the shock wave continues to expand, it enters the structure, pushing both upward on the ceilings and downward on the floors.

Floor failure is common in large-scale vehicle-delivered explosive attacks, because floor slabs typically have a large surface area for the pressure to act on and a comparably small thickness. Floor failure is particularly common for close-in and internal explosions. The loss of a floor system increases the unbraced height of the supporting columns, which may lead to structural instability.

Remember

For hand-carried weapons that are brought into the building and placed on the floor away from a primary vertical load-bearing element, the response will be more localized with damage and injuries extending a bay or two in each direction. Although the weapon is smaller, the air-blast effects are amplified due to multiple reflections from interior surfaces. Typical damage types that may be expected include:

- ☐ localized failure of the floor system immediately below the weapon;
- ☐ damage and possible localized failure for the floor system above the weapon;
- ☐ damage and possible localized failure of nearby concrete and masonry walls;
- ☐ failure of nonstructural elements such as partition walls, false ceilings, ductwork, window treatments; and flying debris generated by furniture, computer equipment, and other contents.

More extensive damage, possibly leading to progressive collapse, may occur if the weapon is strategically placed directly against a primary load-bearing element such as a column.

In comparison to other hazards such as earthquake or wind, an explosive attack has several distinguishing features.

The intensity of the localized pressures acting on building components can be several orders of magnitude greater than these other hazards. It is not uncommon for the peak pressure on the building from a vehicle weapon parked along the curb to be in excess of 100 psi. Major damage and failure of building components is expected even for relatively small weapons, in close proximity to the building.

Explosive pressures decay extremely rapidly with distance from the source. Pressures acting on the building, particularly on the side facing the explosion, may vary significantly, causing a wide range of damage types. As a result, air blast tends to cause more localized damage than other hazards that have a more global effect.

The duration of the event is very short, measured in thousandths of a second, (milliseconds). In terms of timing, the building is engulfed by the shockwave and direct air-blast damage occurs within tens to hundreds of milliseconds from the time of detonation due to the supersonic velocity of the shock wave and the nearly instantaneous response of the structural elements. By comparison, earthquake events last for seconds and wind loads may act on the building for minutes or longer.

Correlation Between Damage And Injuries

Three types of building damage can lead to injuries and possible fatalities.

The most severe building response is collapse. In past incidents, collapse has caused the most extensive fatalities. For the Oklahoma City bombing in 1995, nearly 90 percent of the building occupants who lost their lives were in the collapsed portion of the Alfred P. Murrah Federal Office Building. Many of the survivors in the collapsed region were on the lower floors and had been trapped in void spaces under concrete slabs.

Although the targeted building is at greatest risk of collapse, other nearby buildings may also collapse. For instance, in the Oklahoma City bombing, a total of nine buildings collapsed. Most of these were unreinforced masonry structures that fortunately were largely unoccupied at the time of the attack. In the bombing of the U.S. embassy in Nairobi, Kenya in 1998, the collapse of the Uffundi building, a concrete building adjacent to the embassy, caused hundreds of fatalities.

The collapse of the twin towers of the World Trade Center on September 11, 2001, resulted in 2,750 deaths and debris severely damaged or destroyed more than a dozen adjacent buildings and structures.

Both buildings collapsed symmetrically and more or less straight down, though there was some tilting of the tops of the towers and a significant amount of fallout to the sides. In both cases, the portion of the building that had been damaged by the airplanes failed, which allowed the section above the airplane impacts to fall onto the undamaged structure below. As the collapse progressed, dust and debris could be seen shooting out of the windows several floors below the advancing destruction. The first fragments of the outer walls of the collapsed North Tower struck the ground 9 seconds after the collapse started, and parts of the South Tower after 11 seconds. The lower portions of both buildings' cores (60 stories of WTC 1 and 40 stories of WTC 2) remained standing for up to 25 seconds after the start of the initial collapse before they too collapsed. While they were designed to support enormous static loads, they provided little resistance to the moving mass of the sections above the floors where the collapses initiated. Structural systems respond very differently to static and dynamic loads, and since the motion of the falling portion began as a free fall through the height of at least one story (roughly three meters), the structure beneath them was unable to stop the collapses once they began. Indeed, a fall of only half a meter would have been enough to release the necessary energy to begin an unstoppable collapse.

FEMA completed its performance study of the buildings in May 2002. It declared that the WTC design had been sound, and attributed the collapses wholly to extraordinary factors beyond the control of the builders. While calling for further study, FEMA suggested that the collapses were probably initiated by weakening of the floor joists by the fires that resulted from the aircraft impacts. According to FEMA's report, the floors detached from the main structure of the building and fell onto each other, initiating a progressive "pancake" collapse.

FEMA's early investigation was revised by a later, more detailed investigation conducted by the National Institute of Standards and Technology (NIST), which also consulted outside engineering entities. This investigation was completed in September 2005. Like FEMA, NIST vindicated the design of the WTC, noting that the severity of the attacks and the magnitude of the destruction was beyond anything experienced in U.S. cities in the past. NIST also emphasized the role of the fires, but it did not attribute the collapses to failing floor joists. Instead, NIST found that sagging floors pulled inward on the perimeter columns: "This led to the inward bowing of the perimeter columns and failure of the south face of WTC 1 and the east face of WTC 2, initiating the collapse of each of the towers."

For buildings that remain standing, the next most severe type of injury producing damage is flying debris generated by exterior cladding.

Depending on the severity of the incident, fatalities may occur as a result of flying structural debris. Some examples of exterior wall failure causing injuries are listed below.

In the Oklahoma City bombing, several persons lost their lives after being struck by structural debris generated by infill walls of a concrete frame building in the Water Resources building across the street from the Murrah building.

In the Khobar Towers bombing in 1996, most of the 19 U.S. servicemen who lost their lives were impacted by high velocity projectiles created by the failed exterior cladding on the wall that faced the weapon. The building was an all-precast, reinforced concrete structure with robust connections between the slabs and walls. The numerous lines of vertical support along with the ample lateral stability provided by the "egg crate" configuration of the structural system prevented collapse.

Even if the building remains standing and no structural damage occurs, extensive injuries can occur due to nonstructural damage. Typically, for large-scale incidents, these types of injuries occur to persons who are in buildings that are within several blocks of the incident. Although these injuries are often not life-threatening, many people can be affected, which has an impact on the ability of local medical resources to adequately respond. An example of nonstructural damage causing injuries is the extensive glass lacerations that occurred in the Oklahoma City Bombing within the Regency Towers apartment building, which was approximately 500 feet from the Murrah Building.

In this incident, glass laceration injuries extended as far as 10 blocks from the bombing. Another example is the bombing of the U.S. embassy in Nairobi, Kenya. The explosion occurred near one of the major intersections of the city, which was heavily populated at the time of the bombing, causing extensive glass lacerations to passersby. The ambassador, who was attending a meeting at an office building across from the embassy, sustained an eye injury as a result of extensive window failure in the building.

It is impractical to design a civilian structure to remain undamaged from a large explosion. The protective objectives are therefore related to the type of building and its function. For an office, retail, residential, or light industrial building, where the primary asset is the occupants, the objective is to minimize loss of life. Because of the severity of large scale explosion incidents, the goals are by necessity modest. Moreover, it is recognized that the building will be unusable after the event. This approach is considered a damage-limiting or damage-mitigating approach to design.

Remember To save lives, the primary goals of the design professional are to reduce building damage and to prevent progressive collapse of the building, at least until it can be fully evacuated. A secondary goal is to maintain emergency functions until evacuation is complete.

The design professional is able to reduce building damage by incorporating access controls that allow building security to keep large threats away from the building and to limit charge weights that can be brought into the building.

Preventing the building from collapsing is the most important objective.

Historically, the majority of fatalities that occur in terrorist attacks directed against buildings are due to building collapse. Collapse prevention begins with awareness by architects and engineers that structural integrity against collapse is important enough to be routinely considered in design. Features to improve general structural resistance to collapse can be incorporated into common buildings at affordable cost. At a higher level, designing the building to prevent progressive collapse can be accomplished by the alternate-path method (i.e., design for the building to remain standing following the removal of specific elements) or by direct design of components for air-blast loading.

Furthermore, building design may be optimized by facilitating evacuation, rescue, and recovery efforts through effective placement, structural design, and redundancy of emergency exits and critical mechanical/electrical systems. Through effective structural design, the overall damage levels may be reduced to make it easier for occupants to get out and emergency responders to safely enter.

Beyond the issues of preventing collapse, and facilitating evacuation/rescue the objective is to reduce flying debris generated by failed exterior walls, windows and other components to reduce the severity of injuries and the risk of fatalities. This may be accomplished through selection of appropriate materials and use of capacity-design methods to proportion elements and connections. A well designed system will provide predictable damage modes, selected to minimize injuries.

Finally, good anti-terrorist design is a multidisciplinary effort requiring the concerted efforts of the architect, structural engineer, security professional, and the other design team members. It is also critical for security design to be incorporated as early as possible in the design process to ensure a cost-effective, attractive solution.

Remember

Chemical, Biological, and Radiological Protection

This section discusses three types of air-borne hazards.

1. A large exterior release originating some distance away from the building (includes delivery by aircraft).

2. A small localized exterior release at an air intake or other opening in the exterior envelope of the building.

3. A small interior release in a publicly accessible area, a major egress route, or other vulnerable area (e.g., lobby, mail room, delivery receiving).

Like explosive threats, chemical, biological and radiological (CBR) threats may be delivered externally or internally to the building. External ground-based threats may be released at a standoff distance from the building or may be delivered directly through an air intake or other opening. Interior threats may be delivered to accessible areas such as the lobby, mailroom, or loading dock, or they may be released into a secured area such as a primary egress route.

There may not be an official or obvious warning prior to a CBR event.

While you should always follow any official warnings, the best defense is to be alert to signs of a release occurring near you. The air may be contaminated if you see a suspicious cloud or smoke near ground level, hear an air blast, smell strange odors, see birds or other small animals dying, or hear of more than one person complaining of eye, throat or skin irritation or convulsing.

Chemicals will typically cause problems within seconds or minutes after exposure, but they can sometimes have delayed effects that will not appear for hours or days. Symptoms may include blurred or dimmed vision; eye, throat, or skin irritation; difficulty breathing; excess saliva; or nausea.

Biological and some radioactive contaminants typically will take days to weeks before symptoms appear, so listen for official information regarding symptoms. With radioactive "dirty" bombs, the initial risk is from the explosion. Local responders may advise you to either shelter-in-place or evacuate.

After the initial debris falls to the ground, leaving the area and washing will minimize your risk from the radiation.

Buildings provide a limited level of inherent protection against CBR threats. To some extent, the protection level is a function of how airtight the building is, but to a greater extent it is a function of the HVAC system's design and operating parameters.

The objectives of protective building design as they relate to the CBR threat are first to make it difficult for the terrorist to successfully execute a CBR attack and second, to minimize the impact (e.g., life, health, property damage, loss of commerce) of an attack if it does occur.

In order to reduce the likelihood of an attack, use security and design features that limit the terrorist's ability to approach the building and successfully release the CBR contaminant. Some examples are listed below.

- ☐ Use security stand-off, accessibility, and screening procedures similar to those identified in the explosive threat mitigation section.
- ☐ Recognize areas around HVAC equipment and other mechanical systems to be vulnerable areas requiring special security considerations.
- ☐ Locate outdoor air intakes high above ground level and at inaccessible locations.
- ☐ Prevent unauthorized access to all mechanical areas and equipment.
- ☐ Avoid the use of ground-level mechanical rooms accessible from outside the building. Where such room placement is unavoidable, doors and air vents leading to these rooms should be treated as vulnerable locations and appropriately secured.
- ☐ Treat operable, ground-level windows as a vulnerability and either avoid their use or provide appropriate security precautions to minimize the vulnerability.
- ☐ Interior to the building, minimize public access to HVAC return-air systems.

Air intakes

Air intakes may be made less accessible by placing them as high as possible on the building exterior, with louvers flush with the exterior. All opportunities to reach air-intakes through climbing should be eliminated. Ideally, there is a vertical smooth surface from the ground level to the intake louvers, without such features as high shrubbery, low roofs, canopies, or sunshades, as these features can enable climbing and concealment. To prevent opportunities for a weapon to be lobbed into the intake, the intake louver should be ideally flush with the wall. Otherwise, a surface sloped at least 45 degrees away from the building and further protected through the use of metal mesh (a.k.a. bird screen) should be used. Finally, CCTV surveillance and enhanced security is recommended at intakes.

In addition to providing protection against an air-borne hazard delivered directly into the building, placing air-intakes high above ground provides protection against ground-based standoff threats because the concentration of the air-borne hazard diminishes somewhat with height. Because air-blast pressure decays with height, elevated air intakes also provide modest protection against explosion threats. Furthermore, many recognized sources of indoor air contaminants (e.g., vehicle exhaust, standing water, lawn chemicals, trash, and rodents) tend to be located near ground level. Thus, elevated air intakes are a recommended practice in general for providing healthy indoor air quality.

In the event that a particular air intake does not service an occupied area, it may not be necessary to elevate it above ground level. However, if the unoccupied area is within an otherwise occupied building, the intake should either be elevated or significant precautions (tightly sealed construction between unoccupied/occupied areas, unoccupied area maintained at negative pressure relative to occupied area) should be put in place to ensure that contaminants are unable to penetrate into the occupied area of the building.

Mechanical Areas

Another simple measure is to tightly restrict access to building mechanical areas (e.g., mechanical rooms , roofs, elevator equipment access). These areas provide access to equipment and systems (e.g., HVAC, elevator, building exhaust, and communication and control) that could be used or manipulated to assist in a CBR attack. Additional protection may be provided by including these areas in those monitored by electronic security and by eliminating elevator stops at the levels that house this equipment. For rooftop mechanical equipment, ways of restricting (or at least monitoring) access to the roof that do not violate fire codes should be pursued.

Tips

Return-Air Systems

Similar to the outdoor-air intake, HVAC return-air systems inside the building can be vulnerable to CBR attack. Buildings requiring public access have an increased vulnerability to such an attack. Design approaches that reduce this vulnerability include the use of ducted HVAC returns within public access areas and the careful placement of return-air louvers in secure locations not easily accessed by public occupants. The second objective is to design to minimize the impact of an attack.

For many buildings, especially those requiring public access, the ability to prevent a determined terrorist from initiating a CBR release will be a significant challenge. Compared to buildings in which campus security and internal access can be strictly controlled, public-access buildings may require a greater emphasis on mitigation. However, even private access facilities can fall victim to an internal CBR release, whether through a security lapse or perhaps a delivered product (mail, package, equipment, or food). Examples of design methods to minimize the impact of a CBR attack are listed below.

Public access routes to the building should be designed to channel pedestrians through points of noticeable security presence.

The structural and HVAC design should isolate the most vulnerable public areas (entrance lobbies, mail rooms, load/delivery docks) both physically and in terms of potential contaminant migration.

The HVAC and auxiliary air systems should carefully use positive and negative pressure relationships to influence contaminant migration routes.

Lobbies, Loading Docks, and Mail Sorting Areas

Remember

Vulnerable internal areas where airborne hazards may be brought into the building should be strategically located. These include lobbies, loading docks, and mail sorting areas. Where possible, place these functions outside of the footprint of the main building. When incorporated into the main building, these areas should be physically separated from other areas by floor-to-roof walls. Additionally, these areas should be maintained under negative pressure relative to the rest of the building, but at positive-to-neutral pressure relative to the outdoors. To assist in maintaining the desired pressure relationship, necessary openings (doors, windows, etc.) between secure and vulnerable areas should be equipped with sealing windows and doors, and wall openings due to ductwork, utilities, and other penetrations should be sealed.

Note: Many facilities now use sniffer dogs in and around their loading bays to warn of potential explosive or CBR threats. Sniffer dogs are also being increasingly used in large mails rooms.

Where entries into vulnerable areas are frequent, the use of airlocks or vestibules may be necessary to maintain the desired pressure differentials.

Ductwork that travels through vulnerable areas should be sealed. Ideally, these areas should have separate air-handling units to isolate the hazard. Alternatively, the conditioned air supply to these areas may come from a central unit as long as exhaust/return air from these areas is not allowed to mix into other portions of the building. In addition, emergency exhaust fans that can be activated upon internal CBR release within the vulnerable area will help to purge the hazard from the building and minimize its migration into other areas. Care must be taken that the discharge point for the exhaust system is not co-located with expected egress routes. Consideration should also be given to filtering this exhaust with High Efficiency Particulate Air (HEPA) filtration.

For entrance lobbies that contain a security screening location, it is recommended that an airlock or vestibule be provided between the secured and unsecured areas.

Zoning of HVAC Systems

Large buildings usually have multiple HVAC (heating, ventilation, air conditioning) zones, each zone with its own air-handling unit and duct system. In practice, these zones are not completely separated if they are on the same floor. Air circulates among zones through plenum returns, hallways, atria, and doorways that are normally left open. Depending upon the HVAC design and operation, airflow between zones on different floors can also occur through the intentional use of shared air return/supply systems and through air migrations via stairs and elevator shafts.

Isolating the separate HVAC zones minimizes the potential spread of an airborne hazard within a building , reducing the number of people potentially exposed if there is an internal release. Zone separation also provides limited benefit against an external release, as it increases internal resistance to air movement produced by wind forces and chimney effect, thus reducing the rate of infiltration. In essence, isolating zones divides the building into separate environments, limiting the effects of a single release to an isolated portion of the building. Isolation of zones requires full-height walls between each zone and the adjacent zones and hallway doors.

Remember

Another recommendation is to isolate the return system (i.e., no shared returns). Strategically locate return air grilles in easily observable locations and preferably in areas with reduced public access. Both centralized and decentralized shutdown capabilities are advantageous.

To quickly shut down all HVAC systems at once in the event of an external threat, a single-switch control is recommended for all air exchange fans (includes bathroom, kitchen, and other exhaust sources). In the event of a localized internal release, redundant decentralized shutdown capability is also recommended. Controls should be placed in a location easily accessed by the facility manager, security, or emergency response personnel. Duplicative and separated control systems will add an increased degree of protection. Further protection may be achieved by placing low-leakage automatic dampers on air intakes and exhaust fans that do not already have back-draft dampers.

Tips

Positive Pressurization

Traditional good engineering practice for HVAC design strives to achieve a slight overpressure of 5-12 Pa (.02-inch-.05-inch w.g.) within the building environment, relative to the outdoors. This design practice is intended to reduce uncontrolled infiltration into the building. When combined with effective filtration, this practice will also provide enhanced protection against external releases of CBR aerosols.

Using off-the-shelf technology (e.g., HEPA), manually triggered augmentation systems can be put into place to over-pressure critical zones to intentionally impact routes of contaminant migration and/or to provide safe havens for sheltering-in-place. For egress routes, positive-pressurization is also recommended, unless of course, the CBR source is placed within the egress route. Design parameters for such systems will depend upon many factors specific to the building and critical zone in question. Care must be taken that efforts to obtain a desired pressure relationship within one zone will not put occupants in another zone at increased risk. Lastly, the supply air used to pressurize the critical space must be appropriately filtered (see filtration below) or originate from a non-contaminated source in order to be beneficial.

Air tightness

To limit the infiltration of contaminants from outside the building into the building envelope, building construction should be made as airtight as possible. Tight construction practices (weatherization techniques, tightly sealing windows, doors, wall construction, continuous vapor barriers, sealing interface between wall and window/door frames) will also help to maintain the desired pressure relationships between HVAC zones. To ensure that the construction of the building has been performed correctly, building commissioning is recommended throughout the construction process and prior to taking ownership to observe construction practices and to identify potential airflow trouble spots (cracks, seams, joints, and pores in the building envelope and along the lines separating unsecured from secured space) before they are covered with finish materials.

Filtration Systems

To offer effective protection, filtration systems should be specific to the particular contaminant's physical state and size. Chemical vapor/gas filtration (a.k.a. air cleaning) is currently a very expensive task (high initial and recurring costs) with a limited number of design professionals experienced in its implementation. Specific expertise should be sought if chemical filtration is desired. Possible application of the air cleaning approach to collective protection zones (with emergency activation) can assist in significantly reducing the cost though the protection is limited to the reduced size of the zone.

Most "traditional" HVAC filtration systems focus on aerosol type contaminants.

The CBR threats in this category include radioactive "dirty bombs", bio-aerosols, and some chemical threats. Riot-control agents and low-volatility nerve agents, for example, are generally distributed in aerosol form; however, a vapor component of these chemical agents could pass through a filtration system. HEPA filtration is currently considered adequate by most professionals to achieve sufficient protection from CBR particulates and aerosols. However, HEPA filtration systems generally have a higher acquisition cost than traditional HVAC filters and they cause larger pressure drops within the HVAC system, resulting in increased energy requirements to maintain the same design airflow rate. Due to recent improvements in filter media development, significant improvements in aerosol filtration can be achieved at relatively minimal increases in initial and operating costs. Also important is that incremental increases in filtration efficiency will generally provide incremental increases in protection from the aerosol contaminant. In 1999, the American Society of Heating, Refrigeration, and Air Conditioning Engineers (ASHRAE) released Standard 52.2-1999. This standard provides a system for rating filters that quantifies filtration efficiency in different particle size ranges to provide a composite efficiency value named the Minimum Efficiency Reporting Value (MERV).

MERV ratings range between 1 and 20 with a higher MERV indicating a more efficient filter. Using the MERV rating table, a desired filter efficiency may be selected according to the size of the contaminant under consideration. For example, a filter with a MERV of 13 or more will provide a 90% or greater reduction of most CBR aerosols (generally considered to be at least 1-3 um in size or larger) within the filtered air stream with much lower acquisition and maintenance costs than HEPA filtration.

Efficiency of filtration systems is not the only concern. Air can become filtered only if it actually passes through the filter. Thus, filter-rack design, gasketing, and good quality filter sources should all play a role in minimizing bypass around the filter. The use of return-air filtration systems and the strategic location of supply and return systems should also be carefully employed to maximize effective ventilation and filtration rates.

Detection Systems

Beyond the measures discussed above, there is the option of using detection systems as part of the protective design package. In general, affordable, timely, and practical detection systems specific to all CBR agents are not yet available. However, for aerosol contaminants, nonspecific detection equipment can be employed to activate response actions should a sudden spike in aerosol concentration of a specific size range be detected. If the spike were detected in an outdoor intake for example, this could trigger possible response options such as damper closure, system shutdown, bypass to alternate air intake, or rerouting the air through a special bank of filters. Such protective actions could occur until an investigation was performed by trained personnel (i.e., check with adjacent alarms, and review security tape covering outdoor air intake). Unless foul play was discovered, the entire process could be completed within 10 minutes or less and without alarming occupants. The initial cost of such a system is relatively modest (depending upon the number of detectors and response options incorporated into the design), but the maintenance requirements are relatively high. Similar monitoring systems could be employed to trigger appropriate responses in high-threat areas such as mailrooms, shipping/receiving areas, or entrance lobbies. The approach could also be expanded to incorporate some of the newer chemical detection technologies, though the low threshold requirements may generate a substantial number of false positives. As technology progresses, detector availability and specificity should continue to expand into the general marketplace.

Remember

Emergency Response Using Fire/HVAC Control Center

Certain operations that are managed at the Fire Control Center can play a protective role in the response to a CBR incident. Examples of such operations and how they could be used are given below.

Purge fans. These can be used to purge an interior CBR release or to reduce indoor contaminant concentrations following building exposure to an external CBR source. (Note: In practice, some jurisdictions may recommend purging for chemical and radiological contaminants but not for biological contaminants, which may be communicable and/or medically treatable.)

Communication Systems. Building communication systems that allow specific instructions to be addressed to occupants in specific zones of the building can play a significant role in directing occupant response to either an internal or external release.

Pressurization Fans. These provide two functions. First, the ability to override and deactivate specific positive-pressure zones may be beneficial in the event that a known CBR source is placed into such an area. Second, areas designated for positive pressurization (generally for smoke protection) may also become beneficial havens for protection from internal and external CBR releases, if they are supplied by appropriately filtered air.

HVAC Controls. The ability to simultaneous and individually manipulate operation of all HVAC and exhaust equipment from a single location may be very useful during a CBR event. Individuals empowered to operate such controls must be trained in their use.

The provision of simple floor-by-floor schematics showing equipment locations and the locations of supply and return louvers will aid the utility of this control option.

Elevator Controls. Depending upon their design and operation, the ability to recall elevators to the ground floor may assist in reducing contaminant migration during a CBR event.

Evolving Technologies

Many of the challenges relating to CBR terrorism prevention will be facilitated with the introduction of new technologies developed to address this emerging threat. As vendors and products come to market, it is important that the designer evaluate performance claims with a close level of scrutiny. Vendors should be willing to guarantee performance specs in writing, provide proof of testing (and show certified results) by an independent, reputable lab, and the testing conditions (e.g., flow rate, residence time, incoming concentrations) should be consistent with what would be experienced within the owner's building.

For CBR developments, proof of federal government testing and acceptance may be available.

Checklist

Chemical, Biological & Radiological Protective Measures

☐ Place air intakes servicing occupied areas as high as practically possible (minimum 12 feet above ground). GSA may require locating at fourth floor or above when applicable.

☐ Restrict access to critical equipment.

☐ Isolate separate HVAC zones and return air systems.

☐ Isolate HVAC supply and return systems in unsecured areas.

☐ Physically isolate unsecured areas from secured areas.

☐ Use positive pressurization of primary egress routes, safe havens, and/or other critical areas.

☐ Commission building throughout construction and prior to taking ownership.

☐ Provide redundant, easily accessible shutdown capabilities.

☐ For higher levels of protection, consider using contaminant-specific filtration and detection systems.

☐ Incorporate fast-acting, low-leaking dampers.

☐ Filter both return air and outdoor air for publicly accessible buildings.

☐ Select filter efficiencies based upon contaminant size. Use reputable filter media installed into tight-fitting, gasketed, and secure filter racks.

☐ For higher threat areas (mail room, receiving, reception/screening lobby):

☐ Preferably locate these areas outside the main building footprint.

☐ Provide separate HVAC, with isolated returns capable of 100% exhaust.

☐ Operate these areas at negative pressure relative to secure portion of the building.

☐ Use air-tight construction, vestibules, and air locks if there is high traffic flow.

☐ Consider installation of an emergency exhaust fan to be activated upon suspected internal CBR release.

☐ Lock, secure, access-log, and control mechanical rooms.

☐ In public access areas, use air diffusers and return air grilles that are secure or under security observation.

☐ Zone the building communication system so that it is capable of delivering explicit instructions, and has back-up power.

☐ Create safe zones using enhanced filtration, tight construction, emergency power, dedicated communication systems, and appropriate supplies (food, water, first aid, and personal-protective equipment).

Safe Rooms

Safe Room Criteria

Most rooms can be used as a safe room if they meet the criteria listed below.

Remember

☐ **Accessibility** – The safe room must be rapidly accessible to all people who are to be sheltered. It should be located so that it can be reached in minimum time with minimum outdoor travel. There are no specific requirements for the time to reach a safe room; however, moving to the safe room from the most distant point in the building should take less than two minutes. For maximum accessibility, the ideal safe room is one in which one spends a substantial portion of time during a normal day. The safe room should be accessible to persons with mobility, cognitive, or other disabilities. Appropriate use of stairs or ramps when shelters are located above or below grade must account for such occupants.

☐ **Size** – The size criterion for the toxic-agent safe room is the same as tornado shelters. Per FEMA 361, the room should provide five square feet per standing adult, six square feet per seated adult, and 10 square feet per wheelchair user for occupancy of up to two hours.

☐ **Tightness** – There is no specific criterion for air tightness. With doors closed, the safe room must have a low rate of air exchange between it and the outdoors or the adjacent indoor spaces. Rooms with few or no windows are preferable if the windows are of a type and condition that do not seal tightly (e.g., older sliders). The room must not have lay-in ceilings (suspended tile ceilings) unless there is a hard ceiling above. The room should have a minimum number of doors, and the doors should not have louvers unless they can be sealed quickly. The door undercut must be small enough to allow sealing with a door-sweep weather strip or expediently with duct tape.

☐ **HVAC system** – The safe room must be isolated or capable of being isolated quickly from the HVAC system of the building. If the selected room is served by supply and return ducts, modifications or preparations must include a means of temporarily closing the ducts to the safe room. In the simplest form, this involves placing duct tape or contact paper over the supply, return, and exhaust grilles and turning off fans and air-handling units. If there is a window-type or through-the-wall air conditioner in the selected room, plastic sheeting and tape must be available to place over the inside of the window and/or air conditioner, which must be turned off when sheltering in the safe room.

☐ **Ventilation** – For Class 1 Safe Rooms, 15 cfm per person is the desired ventilation rate; however, the minimum ventilation rate is 5 cfm per person if that rate is adequate for pressurization. Class 3 and unventilated Class 2 Safe Rooms are suitable only for short-duration use, not only because the low ventilation rate when occupied can cause carbon dioxide levels to rise, but also because protection diminishes as the time of exposure to the hazard increases.

☐ **Location** – For unventilated shelters (Class 3 and some Class 2), there are three considerations for location within a building. First, relative to the prevailing wind, the safe room should be on the leeward side of a building. Second, if there is a toxic materials storage or processing plant in the community, the safe room should be on the side opposite the plant. Third, an interior room is preferable to a room with exterior walls, if it meets criteria for size, tightness, and accessibility. For a low-rise building, there is no substantial advantage in a room on the higher floors, and a location should not be selected based on height above ground level if it increases the time required to reach the shelter in an emergency. The location must allow people to get there in a timely fashion and the shelter must be usable year-round.

☐ **Water and toilets** – Drinking water and a toilet(s) should be available to occupants of a safe room. This may involve the use of canned/bottled water and portable toilets. Toilet fixture allowance is presented in FEMA 361.

☐ **Communications** – For sheltering situations initiated by local authorities, the safe room must contain a radio with which to receive emergency instructions for the termination of sheltering. A telephone or cell phone can be used to receive emergency instructions and to communicate with emergency management agencies. Electrical power and lighting are also required.

Safe Rooms in Response to the Domestic Explosive Threat

The concept of safe rooms has been around for quite some time. Bomb shelters were used in the United Kingdom (U.K.) during World War II to protect the civilian populations against aerial attack, and fall-out shelters were established in cities in the United States during the Cold War to protect against the lingering effects of a feared nuclear attack. More recently, the Israeli Defense Force (IDF) requires apartment protected spaces (APSs) or floor protected spaces (FPSs) to be constructed in every new building or to be added to existing buildings according to engineering specifications. In buildings in which no shelters exist, interior rooms may be converted to shelters by following IDF instructions. In all cases, the shelters must be accessible within two minutes of a warning siren. The protected spaces are intended to serve as a refuge when an attack is suspected, either through early warning or remote detection; however, the protected space is much less effective when the event takes place without warning. Two minutes and 11 seconds elapsed between the time the Ryder truck stopped in front of the Murrah Federal Building in Oklahoma City and the detonation of its explosives, but no one was alerted to the danger until the explosion occurred. At Khobar Towers in Dhahran, Saudi Arabia, U.S. Air Force Security Police observers on the roof of the building overlooking the perimeter identified an attack in progress and alerted many occupants to the threat; however, evacuation was incomplete, and 500 people were wounded and 19 people were killed by the explosion.

Remember

The effectiveness of the safe room in protecting occupants from the effects of an explosive detonation is, therefore. highly dependent on early detection and warning. Unless the attacker notifies authorities of a bomb threat, as often occurred in the terrorist activities in Northern Ireland, the safe room can best be used after an explosion occurs in anticipation of a second attack. The 1998 bombing of the U.S. Embassy in Kenya was preceded by a small explosion that drew curious embassy employees to the windows; such a tactic, if repeated in the United States, would justify the relocation of school occupants to a safe room until school officials are able to determine that it is safe to disperse the students. To these limited objectives , the establishment of a safe room in schools may serve a useful purpose. Given the nature of the explosive threat, however, it may be more effective to provide debris mitigating protective measures for all exterior façade elements.

It is important to understand the nature of the domestic explosive threat in order to effectively plan for the protection of different types of facilities and particularly for the establishment of safe rooms in schools. Although the patterns of past events may not predict the future, they give valuable insight to the protection against a very low-probability, but potentially high-consequence, event. As previously discussed, despite a wide range of terrorist events, such as CBR contamination, an explosion remains the most insidious threat, requiring the least sophisticated materials and expertise. The principal components of an explosive device can be obtained at a variety of retail outlets, without arousing suspicion. Every year, over 1,000 intentional explosive detonations are reported by the FBI Bomb Data Center. In 1998, the last year for which the compiled data were published, there were 1,225 actual incidents of unauthorized explosions in the United States. The majority of these explosives were targeted against residential properties and vehicles; however, 76 explosive events were detonated at educational facilities, causing a total of $28,500 in property damage. In addition to these actual events, 63 incidents involving hoax devices were investigated. By contrast, only one explosive device was detonated at a federal government facility, causing $1.5 million in property damage, and eight were detonated at local/state government facilities, causing $316,000 in property damage. Over 70 percent of the people involved in bombing incidents were "young offenders" and less than 1/2 percent were members of terrorist groups. Vandalism was the motivation in 40 percent of the intentional and accidental bombing incidents. Although two out of three attacks were perpetrated between 6 p.m. and 6 a.m., the incidents against educational facilities were more uniformly distributed throughout the day. Although each successive major domestic terrorist event exceeded the intensity of the predecessor, this is not particularly relevant to the threats to which a school structure might be subjected; if an explosive were to be detonated in or around a school building, it would most likely be a small improvised device assembled by a youth, and vandalism is most likely to be the motive.

The size of the explosive that might be considered for a protective design is limited by the maximum weight that might be transported either by hand or by vehicle. Despite the large weight of explosives that might be transported by vehicle, there have been relatively few large-scale explosive events within the United States. The 1995 explosion that collapsed portions of the Murrah Federal Building in Oklahoma City contained 4,800 pounds of ammonium nitrate and fuel oil (ANFO), and the 1993 explosion within the parking garage beneath the World Trade Center complex contained 1,200 pounds of urea nitrate. As implied by the FBI statistics, the majority of the domestic events contain significantly smaller weights of low-energy explosives. The explosive that was used in the 1996 pipe bomb attack at the Olympics in Atlanta consisted of smokeless powder and was preceded by a warning that was called in 23 minutes before the detonation. Nevertheless, the protective design of structures focuses on the effects of high energy explosives and relates the different mixtures to an equivalent weight of trinitrotoluene (TNT).

Locating Safe Rooms to Mitigate Threats

The building's façade is its first real defense against the effects of a bomb and typically the weakest component that would be subjected to blast pressures. Although the response of specific glazed components is a function of the dimensions, make-up, and construction techniques, the conventionally glazed portions of the façade would shatter and inflict severe wounds when subjected to a 50-pound explosive detonation at a stand-off distance of about 200 feet. If the glazed elements are upgraded with a fragment retention film (FRF), the same façade element may be able to withstand a 50-pound explosive detonation at a stand-off distance of about 70 feet. Unreinforced masonry block walls are similarly vulnerable to collapse when subjected to a 50-pound threat at a stand-off distance of 50 feet; however, if these same walls are upgraded with a debris catching system, they may be able to sustain this same intensity explosive detonation at a stand-off distance of 20 feet. If the weight of explosives were increased from 50 pounds to 500 pounds, the required stand-off distances to prevent severe wounds increases to 500 feet for conventional window glazing, 200 feet for window glazing treated with a FRF, 250 feet for unreinforced masonry block walls, and 60 feet for masonry walls upgraded with a debris catching system. Based on these dimensions, it is apparent that substantial stand-off distances are required for the unprotected structure, and these distances may be significantly reduced through the use of debris mitigating retrofit systems. Furthermore, because blast loads diminish with distance and geometry of wave propagation relative to the loaded surface of the building, the larger threats at larger stand-off distances are likely to damage a larger percentage of façade elements than the more localized effects of smaller threats at shorter stand-off distances. Safe rooms that may be located within the school should, therefore, be located in windowless spaces or spaces in which the window glazing was upgraded with a FRF.

Although small weights of explosives are not likely to produce significant blast loads on the roof, low-rise structures may be vulnerable to blast loadings resulting from large weights of explosives at large stand-off distances that may sweep over the top of the building. The blast pressures that may be applied to these roofs are likely to far exceed the conventional design loads and, unless the roof is a concrete deck or concrete slab structure, it may be expected to fail. There is little that can be done to increase the roof's resistance to blast loading that doesn't require extensive renovation of the building structure. Therefore, safe rooms should be located at lower floors, away from the roof debris that may rain down in response to blast loading.

The building's lateral load-resisting system, the structural frame or shear walls that resist wind and seismic loads, will be required to receive the blast loads that are applied to the exterior façade and transfer them to the building's foundation. This load path is typically through the floor slabs that act as diaphragms and interconnect the different lateral resisting elements. The lateral load resisting system for a school building depends, to a great extent, on the type of construction and region. In many cases, low-rise buildings do not receive substantial wind and seismic forces and, therefore, do not require substantial lateral load resisting systems. Because blast loads diminish with distance, a package sized explosive threat is likely to locally overwhelm the façade, thereby limiting the force that may be transferred to the lateral load resisting system. However, the intensity of the blast loads that may be applied to the building could exceed the design limits for most conventional school construction. As a result, the building is likely to be subjected to large inelastic deformations that may produce severe cracks to the structural and nonstructural partitions. There is little that can be done to upgrade the existing school structure to make it more flexible in response to a blast loading that doesn't require extensive renovation of the building. Safe rooms should, therefore, be located close to the interior shear walls or reinforced masonry walls in order to provide maximum structural support.

In addition to the hazard of impact by façade debris propelled into the building or roof damage that may rain down, the occupants may also be vulnerable to much heavier debris resulting from structural damage. Progressive collapse occurs when an initiating localized failure causes adjoining members to be overloaded and fail, resulting in an extent of damage that is disproportionate to the originating region of localized failure. The initiating localized failure may result from a sufficiently sized parcel bomb that is in contact with a critical structural element or from a vehicle-sized bomb that is located at a short distance from the structure. However, a large explosive device at a large stand-off distance is not likely to selectively cause a single structural member to fail; any damage that results from this scenario is more likely to be widespread and the ensuing collapse cannot be considered progressive. Although progressive collapse is not typically an issue for buildings three stories or shorter, transfer girders or precast construction may produce structural systems that are not tolerant of localized damage conditions. The columns that support transfer girders and the transfer girders themselves may be critical to the stability of a large area of floor space. Similarly, precast construction that relies on individual structural panels may not be sufficiently tied together to resist the localized damage or large structural deformations that may result from an explosive detonation. As a result, safe rooms should not be located on a structure that is either supported by or underneath a structure that is supported by transfer girders unless the building is evaluated by a licensed professional engineer. The connection details for multi-story precast structures should also be evaluated before the building is used to house a safe room.

Nonstructural building components (e.g., piping, ducts, lighting units, and conduits) that are located within safe rooms must be sufficiently tied back to a competent structure to prevent failure of the services and the hazard of falling debris. To mitigate the effects of in-structure shock that may result from the infilling of blast pressures through damaged windows, the nonstructural systems should be located below the raised floors or tied to the ceiling slabs with seismic restraints.

Safe Rooms v Protected Spaces

Israel as a Benchmark...

Israel's built environment has been continuously challenged since 1948.

As a nation with minimal resources & confined boundaries, Israel has developed a nation wide building threat mitigation infrastructure:

- ☐ Home Front Command ("Haga") , branch of Israel Defense Force IDF)
- ☐ "Haga" Requirements are integrated in the Israeli Building Codes & Standards ("The Blue Book" - Israel's "UBC")
- ☐ National Communication Network; TV & Radio etc.
- ☐ Nation wide Operational Procedures, Individual Bio/Chem. Protective Kits (IPK) – distribution
- ☐ Military & Security Training (Mandatory military service)
- ☐ People Screening Vs technology
- ☐ Building material & security systems development i.e.; blast proof glazing, building hardening…)
- ☐ National intelligence network (Mosad, Military intelligence, Police, Ministry of Interiors…)

Israel - Vulnerabilities

- ☐ Residential communities
- ☐ Educational facilities - (Pre-K through University)
- ☐ Transportation - Buses & Bus Stations Airports, Sea ports
- ☐ Large gatherings (Independence Day etc.)
- ☐ Commercial centers & malls
- ☐ Recreational open spaces - parks & streets
- ☐ Sport arenas & events
- ☐ Military buildings & installations

- ☐ Businesses centers
- ☐ Government buildings
- ☐ Religious institutions
- ☐ Industrial hazardous Facilities

Israel - terrorist incidents

- ☐ Suicide Bombers
- ☐ Hit & run attacks/ Drive by Shooting
- ☐ Assault / Stabbing
- ☐ Grenades
- ☐ Anti tank Missiles
- ☐ Mortar Bombs
- ☐ Rockets
- ☐ Car bombs
- ☐ Letter bombs
- ☐ Hijacking; soldiers & civilians
- ☐ Missile launches (Scuds etc.)
- ☐ Plane Hijacking
- ☐ Bio /Chem. Threats

The Bomb Shelter Concept

- ☐ Pre 1991: "Direct Hit" was perceived as a high risk (primarily war based 1948, 56, 67, 73, 82).
- ☐ Israel Building Code gave direction to construct Underground Bomb shelters in every building or part of a campus layout.
- ☐ Shelters were sized per occupant load and located on main building exiting systems (Residential, Offices Hospital, Manufacturing.)
- ☐ Bomb Shelter: Underground, 400mm concrete walls, with Steel blast proof Doors & Windows, Exiting tunnels, Air filtration provisions.
- ☐ Layout included: Decontamination, Safety Shower, Water supply, 12 volt lighting, Radio & Antenna connections, Air filtering etc.
- ☐ Shelters were dual use - recreational, (comfortable for long periods of time.)
- ☐ Siren or radio alert - means of communication to go to Bomb Shelter.

Desert Storm War 1991

☐ Operations:

- Early intelligence warnings, Individual Bio/Chem protective Kits (IPK's) distribution (Masks , atropine, etc.)
- Hospital Bio/Chem. ready upgrades & temp field stations.
- Protected Spaces were created in lieu of Underground Bomb Shelters Haga rep.'s gave instructions in the media (seal & tape windows…etc.)
- USA entered Kuwait; Israel was attacked by Iraqi scud missiles
- Operations: Israel was divided into zones (A,B,C etc.)
- Radio was the primary means of communications (IDF spokesman)
- Sirens & radio alert were alarmed with scud missile launch, P.S room was entered & sealed, gas masks on, radio on, await direction...
- communicated which zones were safe to either take of masks or to leave P.S.
- Final all clear signal was given after missile fall was located & identified as non-Bio/Chem.

Overall concept:

☐ Minimize havoc, keep people off the roads & in secured areas connected to the media.

☐ Let the authorized people do their job!

Protected Spaces

Protected Spaces were sized per occupant load & located on each floor(residential, offices, hospitals, Manufacturing etc.)

☐ Floor Protected Space (FPS): Shared area on each floor serving no more than 4 apartments 4-5 square meters per min. apartment.

☐ Apartment Protected Space (APS): 5 square meters min.

☐ Protected Space in new facilities: 200 mm Concrete blast proof walls, HM steel sealed Doors, Polly-carbonate Windows w/ steel shutters, Shatter proof interior finishes.

☐ Existing buildings - modifications creating "safe havens" (sealing windows and doors, using the 2 minute travel distance, geo-tech membrane hardening...)

☐ Multi use Shelters - more like regular rooms w/ minimal limitations to interior finishes; bedrooms, conference rooms, break rooms etc.

☐ Bio/Chem protection: Gas masks, Atropine & other necessary gear is stored in P.S. (Regularly replaced)

"Haga" Today

- ☐ "Haga" is the Israel Defense Force - Home Front Command branch.
- ☐ Haga requirements are an integral part of the Israeli Building code.
- ☐ Home Front Command military engineers issue permits for the Protected Space
- ☐ Sizing & location of Protected Spaces is done at the front end of design, per Haga guidelines. No way around it!
- ☐ Structural; Re-bar detailing of, Door & Window anchoring & calculations must be reviewed & approved prior to receiving building permits.
- ☐ In high rise applications, 75% of Floor Protected Space structure must be vertically continuous.
- ☐ "Haga" permits must be onsite available for review at all times from construction through occupancy.

The Architectural Design Challenges

- ☐ Integration of "Safe Havens" in design.
- ☐ Psyche, how will people react to acts of terror?
- ☐ Sense of security - potential impacts to national productivity.
- ☐ What are the real risks? What is the probability of them occurring?
- ☐ New construction or retrofit.
- ☐ How much down time can different building types live with?
- ☐ Building security product development.
- ☐ The architect's role in fitting the systems in!
- ☐ Means of communications during an event, accountability!
- ☐ Operational assessments - People factor, training & screening, everyone is a security guard, eyes & ears.
- ☐ Bunkers Vs wide open spaces
- ☐ Avoidance Vs Mitigation
- ☐ Insurance carriers lead the design?

The US Situation

- ☐ 911 was a catalyst,
- ☐ Paradigm shift: From probability if to probability when & where.

☐ Current Benchmarks for terrorist threat mitigation in the USA are primarily DOD based specifically created for the design of Embassies, Consulates & other Federal or Military installations.

☐ UBC & UFC guidelines are focused on threat to life & property, mitigating; Fire, Earthquakes, & other natural hazards.

☐ Building security design criteria in the private sector is typically driven by insurance carriers or threats perceived by owners (to residents, products, information & property)

☐ Currently minimal standards are in place for mitigating the new threats to the built environment for existing or new facilities

Next Steps?

☐ Categorize building types - National level of urgency.

☐ Case Studies - per building type, creating nation-wide benchmarks. (1st Lifelines; Airports, Hospitals, Dams etc.; 2nd Industrial, commercial, residential...etc.)

☐ Standardization of new guidelines per building type.

☐ Building Code Modifications?

☐ Fast track Risk Assessment

☐ Site

☐ Buildings

☐ Systems

☐ Facility Operations

☐ Prioritization of the identified vulnerabilities.

☐ Mitigation plans per identified threats to our built environment.

☐ Ongoing training / Education & lessons learned...

Commercial Retail Space Occupancy- Explosive And CBR Threats

Commercial retail space such as malls, movie theatres, hotels, night clubs, casinos, and other spaces that house large public populations gathering for shopping or entertainment have their own unique features that increase their vulnerability compared with that of office buildings.

Often, these spaces are low-rise buildings that have large interior spaces with high, laterally unsupported walls, long-span roofs, and interior columns spaced relatively far apart. They are generally constructed using lightweight construction and may be prefabricated. This type of construction has little if any redundancy, which increases the structural vulnerability significantly.

Remember

The primary goal for this type of construction is to prevent progressive collapse of the building in response to a large-scale attack. Where possible, floor-to-floor height and bay spacing should be reduced, and lateral bracing of the columns and roof joists should be provided. Connections should be designed to be at least as strong as the members. Secondary structural framing systems further enhance protection. To limit laceration injuries, lamination of glass is recommended. Consider structural partition walls or shelving units placed within the space that will stop the roof system from falling directly on the occupants in the event of collapse. If this approach is used, take care that the partitions have sufficient lateral support so that they do not topple over.

Tips

In these large spaces, it is virtually impossible to isolate HVAC to protect against CBR-type threats. In this case, negative zone pressurization or smoke-evacuation methods become critically important. Also, mechanical areas should be protected with restricted access and a hardened shell (walls, ceiling and floor). It is also recommended to have centralized redundant control stations, easily accessible by appropriate personnel.

Consideration should be given to providing additional, clearly marked, easily located egress routes to facilitate mass evacuation. If there are business offices serving these buildings with a sizable workforce, consider relocating these and other mixed-use functions to a separate, offsite location.

Light Industrial Buildings

Light industrial buildings are used throughout the United States for offices, light manufacturing, laboratories, warehouses, and other commercial purposes. Typically, these buildings are low-rise buildings three to five stories high, often using tilt-up concrete construction. Typically, they are located in industrial or commercial complexes and may have significant setbacks from public streets. They are serviced by surface parking lots or parking structures outside the building. Security may vary widely depending on the use of the building. For a building used for laboratories or manufacturing, there may already be significant security measures at the perimeter and inside the building. For office buildings, security may be light to negligible.

The main focus of this section is on light industrial buildings that house office space, because these are the buildings with potentially high populations, and therefore, life safety is a primary concern. For warehouses and manufacturing plants, the primary objective is more likely to be protection of the contents and processes. For laboratories, the primary objectives are to prevent release or deflagration of hazardous materials and to protect processes.

Office parks inherently have an open character with medium-to-large setbacks from the street and public parking. In this environment, the most effective way to protect the building from moving vehicle threats is to use landscaping methods between public streets and parking to prevent the intrusion of vehicles. Devices such as ponds, fountains, berms, and ditches can be very effective in reducing the accessibility of the building exterior to high-speed vehicles.

Parking should be placed as far as practical from the building. Driveways leading directly to the building entrance should have a meandering path from the public streets that does not permit high velocities to be achieved. Separation between the driveway and building may be achieved through a number of devices such as a pond with a bridge leading to the entrance, a knee wall with foliage in front, or other landscape features.

The design of parking structures servicing these buildings should fulfill two main objectives to prevent explosions in the parking structure from seriously damaging the main office building. The first is to control the lines of sight between the parking structure and the building to limit air-blast effects on the building. One solution is to use a solid wall that is bermed and landscaped on the side of the parking structure facing the building. Second, design the parking structure to withstand the design level explosion without structural failure in order to reduce the potential for debris from a parking structure failure damaging the office building. This second objective can be achieved while still allowing the parking structure to sustain significant levels of damage.

For the tilt-up walls, use continuous vertical reinforcement with staggered splices, preferably on both sides of the wall to resist large lateral loads. It may be advantageous to consider designs that permit the wall to bear against floor diaphragms to resist loads. Connections between the walls and structural frame should be able to accept large rebound forces to prevent the wall from being pulled off the exterior. Care should be taken to prevent the wall from bearing directly against exterior columns to limit the opportunity for progressive collapse. Using laminated glass on the exterior reduces the potential for laceration injuries. For the roof, a concrete slab with or without decking is preferred over a solution using metal decking only.

Summary

Having read through this chapter you can see the vast array of options that are available to you. Remember that there is no one solution for all. Your facility has very specific functions and the strategic security plan that you develop for your particular needs may not be exactly the same as a similar facility across the road. The purpose of the assessment process is to identify the systems and devices that are most relevant to your needs and circumstances. Deciding what is right for you is a lengthy analytical process with frequent re-assessments to ensure you are creating the most cost-effective and appropriate solution.

Remember

However, the more help you can get during this process, the more comprehensive it will be. You are not alone. There is a wealth of expertise available to you. Consult with your fire and police departments and your local and state emergency management personnel. Discuss your plans with your insurance agent. The implementation of a physical security system may reduce your premiums and in some, cases the insurers may even be willing to contribute towards the cost if it significantly reduces their liability. Consult with security experts and security designers if you have special needs and finally, communicate with neighboring facilities whether in the same line of business as you or not. Eventually, if a national dialogue can be developed, information can be shared, best practices developed and we will all be safer and more secure as a result.

Before proceeding to the next chapter make sure you are familiar with all your preferred options and how they all will work together to meet your physical security needs and objectives. Now proceed to the next chapter to create your own integrated physical security plan.

STEP FOUR: SECURITY STRATEGIC PLAN

Introduction

Now that you have identified and prioritized your facility's security vulnerabilities the next task is to prepare a comprehensive integrated physical security strategic plan that will be the basis for executing security upgrades at your facility. Like any other strategic plan it must be a living document that is presented to facility/company management and fully integrated in the overall corporations program. Your goal is to integrate facility security both in the short term and the long term. In the short term your aim is to upgrade facility security but in the long term you have to appreciate that this is just one more element - albeit a very important one – in the overall program mission.

Must Do

Why do I need a strategic plan?

The WHY, WHAT & WHEN

The strategic plan serves a number of important functions. You know what you want to do and you have to get both the budget and the go-ahead to do it – that is where the strategic plan comes in. Without it you will not move to the next step of implementation.

The plan is the marketing tool you need to get management approval. It is the blueprint for your physical security plan and it focuses your attention on exactly what it is that you want to achieve.

Before continuing, you must identify and document your goals – what do you want your integrated physical security plan to achieve i.e. "I want to maximize security with minimal impact to facility operations."

Tips

As you proceed to write your integrated physical security plan you are documenting WHY changes are necessary in order to meet your goals. Your justification for change is your Gap Analysis. The scope of WHAT needs to be done is determined by your Gap Closure analysis and assessment.

The Integrated Physical Security Handbook

Recognizing that some change is unavoidable, especially during implementation, you and your team will conduct an impact analysis as part of the plan. For every change recommended by your Gap Closure analysis, determine what impact – cost and operational - there might be both in the short term –during implementation – and in the long term – after commissioning.

Finally, the strategic plan will set out a schedule for implementation – WHEN the work will be done, how it will be done and who will be responsible for what.

Checklist

The following items are key components of strategic plans:

☐ Mission Statement (what we do)

☐ Vision Statement (what we need to do to protect it)

☐ Budget

☐ Timeline

☐ Organizational Values

☐ Identification of Critical/Strategic Issues (Justification for action)

☐ Identification of critical assets

☐ Identification of risks and vulnerabilities

☐ Identification of risks

☐ Strategic Areas of Emphasis/Goals with Strategic Statement/Recommended Actions for each Issue or Goal

☐ Measures of Success

☐ Multi-year Action Plans (Action Goals)

Developing Your Integrated Physical Security Strategic Plan

Having analyzed your facility and its operations, identified critical assets, threats and vulnerabilities and considered all your options, you and your team are now ready to put together your integrated physical security strategic plan.

Checklist

To write the strategic plan, the Team should have a vulnerability portfolio available. This portfolio should include the following:

☐ Assessment agenda

☐ Assessment background information (collected by the Assessment Team and building owners

☐ Threats rating

☐ Asset value ranking worksheet

☐ Key documents (plans, procedures, and policies)

☐ Emergency procedures (baseline organization response and recovery capability in case of an attack or event)

168   www.GovernmentTrainingInc.com

☐ Building Vulnerability Assessment Checklist

☐ Risk assessment matrices

Key Issues

Before continuing it is worth recapping, as part of our strategic planning, some of the issues raised from your Gap Analysis.

Core Team

During the process of conducting all your facility assessments, you will already have discovered who the key people are that you need in your strategic planning team. The team should be composed of senior individuals who have a breadth and depth of experience and understand other disciplines and system interdependencies.

The Team leader/project manager will work with the team, building owner and stakeholders to:

☐ Determine the asset value

☐ Determine the threat rating

☐ Determine the level of protection

The Team will coordinate the preparation of an assessment schedule, assessment agenda, and on-site visit assessments with the building stakeholders. It is important to emphasize that your Team should be composed of people capable of evaluating different parts of the buildings and with expertise in engineering, architecture, IT, maintenance, operations, site planning and so on. Other members of the team may include law-enforcement agents, first responders, and building owners and managers. If you create a security focused core team that includes different end users and facility maintenance staff you will come up with working solutions versus good ideas that won't be implemented.

Make a list of managers/experts who can collectively bring together all the knowledge you need to develop your strategic plan:

Core Team	Name	Contact Information	Specific role
Project Manager			
IT			
Security			
Physical Security			
Facility Operations			
HVAC			
Procedural Guidelines			
Compliance (legal/regulatory)			

Core Team	Name	Contact Information	Specific role
Security Consultant			
Fire			
Police			
Insurance			
Others			

Involve Senior Management

Must Do

You must get management buy in so involve senior management in the process from the start. They must be responsible for driving the change process and understanding the reasons for it.

This is a critical step in establishing a strong internal security culture.

Keep People Informed

Ensure that everyone who needs to know understands what is going on and why changes are going to take place. Make sure they know the reasons for the security changes and how they will be benefit from them i.e. they will be safer. Managing this change is important to prevent disruption in the workforce and if you can staff, tenants and other stakeholders to buy in at this stage it will be easier to get them to take part in training and drills once the measures have been implemented.

Consult Other Facilities

It makes sense to communicate and consult with other facilities that perform a similar function. They may have already been through this process and can tell you of mistakes to be avoided. It is through this ongoing communication and judicious sharing information that benchmark systems can be developed.

Consult the Consultants

Get the specialists involved as early as possible. This is their area of expertise and it is better to have their advice from day one rather than bring them in late in the day only to have them tell all the things that you shouldn't have done!

- ☐ Identify all critical assets
- ☐ (Refer to Critical Asset checklist in Gap Analysis)
- ☐ Identify all threats and vulnerabilities
- ☐ (Refer to threat and vulnerability assessments checklist)

"What If" scenarios

As part of the strategic plan you must develop multiple "what if" scenarios to cover as many diverse situations that you and the team can think of. Imagine the unimaginable – the very worse case scenarios. What would be the impact if it did happen, how might the incident unfold, what would be the consequences – what are the gaps in your security. Then re-enact the scenario and see what measures could have prevented it or mitigated the impact – what needs to be done to close the gaps. Remember, these measures should include operational and procedural procedures as well as physical security.

Remember

Physical security covers all the devices, technologies and specialist materials for perimeter, external and internal protection. This covers everything from sensors and close circuit television to barriers, lighting and access controls.

Operational procedures are the lifeblood of any organization - they cover how the facility works on a day to day basis, shift changes, deliveries, when maintenance is carried out and so on. You must understand how the facility works and operates in order to develop an effective physical security plan that allows it to get on with its job with the least disruption as possible.

Remember

Equally you must recognize that any effective PSS is going to impact on operations – things will change and you have to both manage and plan for change and ensure that the reasons for the changes are understood and accepted by all personnel.

Procedural security measures spell out who does what and the actions to be taken to prevent an attack or incident, or one should take place to mitigate its impact and ensure continuation of business.

Also, the measures should meet your deter, detect, delay and response criteria – the foundations on which any integrated physical security system must be built.

Deterrence provides countermeasures, such as policies, procedures, and technical devices and controls to defend against attacks on the assets being protected.

Detection monitors for potential breakdowns in protective mechanisms that could result in security breaches.

Delay - if there is a breach, measures are needed to delay the intruders long enough to allow a security team to apprehend them before they achieve their objective.

Response, which requires human involvement, covers procedures and actions for responding to a breach. Note: Because absolute protection is impossible to achieve, a security program that does not also incorporate detection, delay and response is incomplete. To be effective, all three concepts must be elements of a cycle that work together continuously.

We have added the two additional elements because while they are not strictly mitigation, they are the reason you have an integrated physical security plan in the first place.

Recovery is your plan to continue business and operations as normally as possible following an incident. Mitigation planning is part of your response and recovery with the aim of minimizing the effects of any incident.

Re-assessment is crucial and is an ongoing process. Before implementing any changes, revisit your strategic plan to ensure that goals and objectives will be met. Whenever there are changed circumstances or when new threats are identified, revisit your strategic plan and conduct a re-assessment to see what additional measures, if any, are needed.

No No There is no point in spending money on expensive perimeter fences if there is no detection system in place to warn of intrusion. There is no point in installing sophisticated detection systems if there is nobody around to respond to them if they trigger an alarm. And, there is little point in having deterrence and detection without delay if an intruder can gain access, cause damage and get away because there were no delaying measures in place or response times were too slow.

In developing your solutions, you must also be aware of your interdependencies. Your facility does not operate in isolation. It receives deliveries and may send out shipments. Your staff travel in and out, you have visitors and vehicle traffic may pass through your facility or close to it. You are also at risk from neighboring plants that may be high-risk targets or conduct high-risk operations i.e. gas storage facility. You must understand how these downstream-upstream elements might impact on you and you should establish relationships with them as part of your physical security plan. Another consequence of these interdependencies is that you need to come up with secondary impact response plans. I may not be the target but what happens if the gas storage facility blows up, either as a result of a terrorist attack or after being struck by lightning. I need to plan for this eventuality.

These key issues are all relevant to your Gap Closure analysis, all of which are integral to formulating your strategic plan.

Determining Mitigation Options

Less Protection

Less Cost

Less Effort

- Place trash receptacles as far away from the building as possible.
- Remove any dense vegetation that may screen covert activity.
- Use thorn-bearing plant materials to create natural barriers.
- Identify all critical resources in the area (fire and police stations, hospitals, etc.).
- Identify all potentially hazardous facilities in the area (nuclear plants, chemical labs, etc.).
- Use temporary passive barriers to eliminate straight-line vehicular access to high-risk buildings.
- Make proper use of signs for traffic control, building entry control, etc. Minimize signs identifying high-risk areas.
- Introduce traffic calming techniques, including raised crosswalks, speed humps and speed tables, pavement treatments, bulbouts, and traffic circles.
- Identify, secure, and control access to all utility services to the building.
- Limit and control access to all crawl spaces, utility tunnels, and other means of under building access to prevent the planting of explosives.
- Utilize Geographic Information Systems (GIS) to assess adjacent land use.
- Provide open space inside the fence along the perimeter
- Locate fuel storage tanks at least 100 feet from all buildings.
- Block sight lines through building orientation, landscaping, screening, and landforms.
- Use temporary and procedural measures to restrict parking and increase stand-off.
- Locate and consolidate high-risk land uses in the interior of the site.
- Select and design barriers based on threat levels.
- Maintain as much stand-off distance as possible from potential vehicle bombs.
- Separate redundant utility systems.
- Conduct periodic water testing to detect waterborne contaminants.
- Enclose the perimeter of the site. Create a single controlled entrance for vehicles (entry control point).
- Establish law enforcement or security force presence.
- Install quick connects for portable utility backup systems.
- Install security lighting.
- Install closed circuit television cameras.
- Mount all equipment to resist forces in any direction.
- Include security and protection measures in the calculation of land area requirements.
- Design and construct parking to provide adequate stand-off for vehicle bombs.
- Position buildings to permit occupants and security personnel to monitor the site.
- Do not site the building adjacent to potential threats or hazards.
- Locate critical building components away from the main entrance, vehicle circulation, parking, or maintenance area. Harden as appropriate.
- Provide a site-wide public address system and emergency call boxes at readily identified locations.
- Prohibit parking beneath or within a building.
- Design and construct access points at an angle to oncoming streets.
- Designate entry points for commercial and delivery vehicles away from high-risk areas.
- In urban areas with minimum stand-off, push the perimeter out to the edge of the sidewalk by means of bollards, planters, and other obstacles. In extreme cases, push the line farther outward by restricting or eliminating parking along the curb, eliminating loading zones, or through street closings. For this measure, you need to work with your local officials.
- Provide instrusion detection sensors for all utility services to the building.
- Provide redundant utility systems to support security, life safety, and rescue functions.
- Conceal and/or harden incoming utility systems.

Greater Protection

Greater Cost

Greater Effort

Mitigation Options for the Second Layer of Defense

Less Protection

Less Cost

Less Effort

- Install active vehicle crash barriers. Ensure that exterior doors into inhabited areas open outward.. Ensure emergency exit doors only facilitate exciting.
- Secure roof access hatches from the interior. Prevent public access to building roofs.
- Restrict access to building operation systems.
- Conduct periodic training of HVAC operations and maintenance staff.
- Evaluate HVAC control options.
- Install empty conduits for future security control equipment during initial construction of major renovation.
- Do not mount plumbing, electrical fixtures, or utility lines on the inside of exterior walls.
- Minimize interior glazing near high-risk areas.
- Establish emergency plans, policies, and procedures.
- Establish written plans for evacuation and sheltering in place.
- Illuminate building access points.
- Restrict access to building information.
- Secure HVAC intakes and mechanical rooms.
- Limit the number of doors used for normal entry/egress.
- Lock all utility access openings.
- Provide energy power for emergency lighting in restrooms, egress routes, and any meeting room without windows.
- Install an internal public address systems.
- Stagger interior doors and offset interior and exterior doors.
- Eliminate hiding places.
- Install an second and separate telephone service.
- Install radio telemetry distributed antennas throughout the facility.
- Use a badge identification system for building access.
- Install a CCTV surveillance system.
- Install an electronic security alarm system.
- Install rapid response and isolation features into HVAC systems.
- Use interior barriers to differentiate levels of security.
- Locate utility systems away from likely areas of potential attack.
- Install call buttons at key public contact areas.
- Install emergency and normal electric equipment at different locations.
- Avoid exposed structural elements.
- Reinforce foyer walls.
- Use architectural features to deny contact with exposed primary vertical load members.
- Isolate lobbies, mailrooms, loading docks, and storage areas.

Greater Protection

Greater Cost

Greater Effort

- Locate stairwells remotely. Do not discharge stairs into lobbies, parking, or loading areas.
- Elevate HVAC fresh-air intakes.
- Create "shelter-in-place" rooms or areas.
- Separate HVAC zones. Eliminate leaks and increase building air tightness.
- Install blast-resistant doors or steel doors with steel frames.
- Physically separate unsecured areas from the main building.
- Install HVAC exhausting and purging systems.
- Connect interior non-load bearing walls to structure with non-rigid connections.
- Use structural design techniques to resist progressive collapse.

Mitigation Options for the Third Layer of Defense

Less Protection

Less Cost

Less Effort

- Treat exterior shear walls as primary structures.
- Orient glazing perpendicular to the primary facade facing uncontrolled vehicle approaches.
- Use reinforced concrete wall systems in lieu of masonry or curtain walls.
- Ensure active fire system is protected from single-point failure in case of a blast event.

Greater Protection

Greater Cost

Greater Effort

- Install a Backup Control Center (BCC).
- Avoid eaves and overhangs or harden to withstand blast effects.
- Establish ground floor elevation 4 feet above grade.
- Avoid re-entrant corners on the building exterior.

Solutions

Your solutions must be:

☐ Sensible and sustainable

☐ Flexible, upgradeable and adaptable

☐ Compatible

☐ Integrated

Must Do Facilities by definition are budget challenged, therefore any impacts to facility expenditure or to operations is likely to be challenged. You have to prove that the costs are justified and that the preferred solutions meet your security objectives and goals.

You must ensure that the solutions are flexible enough so that they can be adapted or upgraded to accommodate changing circumstances and threats.

You must also ensure that your solutions are compatible for the facility. A fence topped with barbed wire is not an aesthetically pleasing way to protect an art gallery, no matter how effective it might be at keeping art thieves out. Make sure that your security, while still meeting security standards, is compatible with the facility appearance.

You must absolutely ensure that all systems – physical security, IT, utilities and so on – are all fully integrated. If your organization hasn't already done so, develop a comprehensive IT security plan and ensure it is compatible with and can be integrated with your physical security plan. You must also make sure that all personnel security requirements are met.

These are all reason why the strategic plan is so important – it documents the changes needed and provides the rationale – the justification - for them. You can give further weight to your proposals by utilizing security consultants to conduct lifecycle analysis on your security proposals.

Don't assume that you always have to spend money in order to bring about change and enhance your security. Look for ways to tie into existing systems instead of replacing with new ones. Look at implementing baseline level security with upgraded systems only where necessary rather than opting for large blanket solutions.

And, as we have stressed throughout, always balance physical protection systems with operational procedures. Security awareness & training goes a long way.

When developing solutions, your first priority must be to address immediate security vulnerabilities. This does not mean a knee jerk reaction and a bad solution that you will have to live with for the long run.

Rather, develop a phased approach. Develop temporary yet effective maximum security solutions to address your immediate vulnerabilities. These temporary solutions can be phased out as your comprehensive security design is implemented. Remember that wherever possible, your solutions should include built in redundancy.

Your solutions have to be effective and this means revisiting your plans regularly to ensure your goals are still being met. Have there been changes – internal or external or both – that affect functions or operating procedures. Are there new threats and vulnerabilities that need to be addressed?

Remember

Your solutions also have to be legal. Validate if the changes you plan to make will impact existing contracts with internal and external affiliates. Will the changes meet industry standards and be in compliance with regulatory measures.

Regulatory measures include legal, insurance, human resources and other regulatory instruments. Examples include:

- ☐ Legislation that organizes and distributes responsibilities to protect a community from manmade threats
- ☐ Regulations that reduce the financial and social impact of manmade hazards through measures, such as insurance
- ☐ New or updated design and construction codes
- ☐ New or modified land use and zoning regulations
- ☐ Incentives that provide inducements for implementing mitigation measures

In most cases, regulatory measures should be considered before implementing other measures because regulatory measures provide the framework for decision-making, organizing, and financing of mitigation actions.

And above all, as you develop and document your security strategic plan make sure it is safe. Institute a confidentiality policy and make sure that everyone involved in the process is briefed on it. It should cover the confidentiality of the plan itself, the procedures for protecting other critical documentation and clear guidelines on what information will be shared and with whom.

While it is crucial to maintain confidentiality – you don't want your strategic plan falling into the wrong hands – it is also important to keep all interested stakeholders informed about what is going on. This information flow is a critical element for the success of the security program because people need to know in general terms what is happening and why the security changes are to their benefit.

Other points to consider:

In order to identify, select, and implement the most appropriate mitigation measures, general mitigation goals and objectives, and the merits of each potential mitigation measure should be examined. The building owner may take the final decision regarding which mitigation measures should be implemented. However, engineers, architects, landscape architects, and other technical people must be involved in this process to ensure that the results of the risk assessment are met with sound mitigation measures that will increase the capability of the building to resist potential terrorist attacks and other incursions.

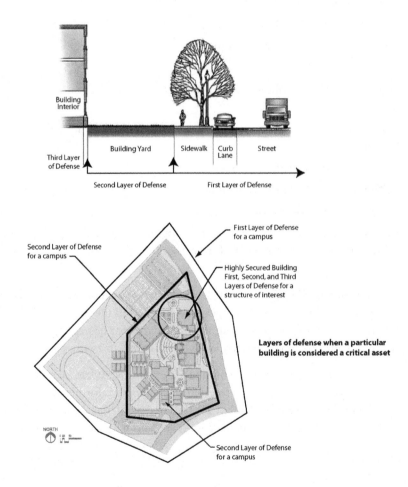

Layers of defense when a particular building is considered a critical asset

Repair and Strengthening of Existing Structures. As its name implies, repair and strengthening deals with structural and non-structural modifications of existing buildings and infrastructure facilities. Although new construction can include protective measures to reduce the potential impact against terrorist attacks, existing buildings may be at risk because they were constructed without the appropriate safety measures to withstand potential terrorist attacks. Thus, improving the safety and structural integrity of existing buildings and infrastructure facilities is often the best way to reduce the impact of manmade events on such structures.

When a manmade hazard occurs, it can directly damage a target building or indirectly cause secondary effects in adjacent buildings. The level of damage is impacted by each structure's quality of design and construction. Poorly engineered and constructed buildings are usually not able to resist the forces generated by a blast event or serve as safe havens in case of CBR attacks.

Protective and Control Measures. Unlike other mitigation measures that improve the resistance of buildings and infrastructure to disasters, protective and control measures focus on protecting structures by deflecting the destructive forces from vulnerable structures and people.

Ideally, a potential terrorist attack is prevented or pre-empted through intelligence measures. If the attack does occur, physical security measures combine with operational forces (e.g., surveillance, guards, and sensors) to provide layers of defense that delay and/or thwart the attack. Deception may be used to make the facility appear to be a more protected or lower-risk facility than it actually is, thereby making it a less attractive target. Deception can also be used to misdirect the attacker to a portion of the facility that is non-critical. As a last resort, structural hardening is provided to save lives and facilitate evacuation and rescue by preventing building collapse and limiting flying debris. Because of the interrelationship between physical and operational security measures, it is imperative for the owner and security professional to define, early in the design process, what extent of operational security is planned for various threat levels.

Available Support

Support involves examining the proposed mitigation options by seeking the opinions of local and State elected officials, as well as the community as a whole. Most communities have learned that success of mitigation efforts hinges on political- and community-wide support. Building an effective political constituency for implementation of mitigation measures in most cases requires time and patience. However, some mitigation options will garner such support more easily than others.

Community Involvement and Acceptance

Remember Community acceptance cannot be viewed separately from the need for political support for the proposed mitigation options. Both are necessary preconditions for their successful implementation. In many cases, community- wide campaigns are necessary to explain the risks, the reasons for, and the expected benefits from the proposed measures.

Cost

Although the implementation of mitigation measures hinges on political commitment and technical capacity, it also depends heavily on the costs involved. After identifying your mitigation measures, you will have some idea of the cost involved and opportunities for implementation.

Benefit

When implementing a mitigation measure, it is important to consider that the benefit of implementing the option outweighs the cost. After identifying your mitigation measures, you will have some idea of the benefits that may result from implementing your mitigation measures.

Available Financial Resources

It is important to have some knowledge of the available resources for implementing mitigation options. The Team should discuss this issue with the site and building owners because the amount of financial resources may define the type of mitigation options to be adopted. The Team should also discuss any Federal and State programs available for financing large-scale mitigation measures.

Legal Authority

Without the appropriate legal authority, a mitigation action cannot lawfully be undertaken. You will need to determine whether the building owner has the legal authority to implement the selected mitigation options or whether it is necessary to wait for new laws or regulations. For example, creating standoff distances in urban areas can be against zoning ordinances and building set-back requirements.

Human Resources Regulations and Laws

There is a wide gamut of HR regulations and laws that have to be complied with from Occupational Safety and Health, to Immigration Control, Employment Laws, Anti-Discrimination and Civil Rights Acts – and everything in between. A fine line has to be walked between providing adequate safety and security for staff and visitors to a building and crossing that line and infringing personal rights and freedoms.

Americans with Disabilities Act (ADA)

The ADA is a wide-ranging civil rights law that prohibits, under certain circumstances, discrimination based on disability. It affords similar protections against discrimination to Americans with disabilities as the Civil Rights Act of 1964, which made discrimination based on race, religion, sex, national origin, and other characteristics illegal. Disability is defined by the ADA as "a physical or mental impairment that substantially limits a major life activity." There is also a requirement on the part of the employer to create "accessibility" – that is to provide products, devices, services and environments that can be accessed by as many people as possible.

Adversely Affected Population

While implementing your mitigation measures to solve problems related to blast and CBR resistance, you may want to consider that some segments of the population may be adversely affected. For example, the construction of barriers and bollards can inhibit the number of tourists visiting a particular city and might affect the community and the hospitality sector.

Remember

Adverse Effects on the Already Built Environment

Some mitigation measures may have a negative effect on the already built environment. When selecting mitigation measures, the following should be strictly scrutinized:

☐ Effects on traffic/vehicular mobility

☐ Effects on pedestrian mobility

☐ Effects on ingress and egress to the building

☐ Effects on other building operations

☐ Effects on aesthetics

☐ Potential interference with first responders

☐ Impact on the Environment

When considering mitigation options, it is important to consider whether the recommended mitigation options will have a negative effect on environmental assets such as threatened and endangered species, wetlands, and other protected natural resources.

Technical Capacity

Some mitigation measures require highly skilled and specialized engineering expertise for implementation. Although experts can be hired on a short-term basis, the technical complexity of some mitigation solutions may require the expertise for long-term maintenance. It is therefore necessary to examine the technical capacities of all stakeholders and identify key technical expertise needed for each proposed mitigation option. If adequate technical capabilities are available for proposed mitigation measures, you should rank them higher on your priority list.

Funding for Maintenance and Operations

When considering the implementation of your mitigation options, you should be sure that funding is available for maintenance and operations.

Ease and Speed of Implementation

Different mitigation measures require different kinds of authority for their implementation. The Team must identify public authorities and responsible agencies for implementing mitigation measures and must examine their rules and regulations. The Team must identify all legislative problem areas and institutional obstacles as well as the incentives that can facilitate mitigation and implementation. The Team will have to balance the desirability of the mitigation measure against the community's rules and regulations in order to decide which takes precedence.

Timeframe and Urgency

Remember

Some mitigation measures require immediate implementation due to their nature (i.e., repetitive security breaches), political desire (i.e., platform project), or social perception (i.e., recent damage and disaster) of the risk. These perceptions can be the drivers to determining the timeframe for implementation of your mitigation options.

Short-term Solutions/Benefits

When considering your mitigation options, you may want to evaluate your short-term solutions (i.e., mitigation options that will solve a particular problem temporarily, but may require additional funding in the future for follow-on projects). A short-term solution can be quickly accomplished and can demonstrate immediate progress in satisfying your community needs.

Long-term Solutions/Benefits

When considering your mitigation options, you may want to evaluate your long-term solutions (i.e., mitigation options that cannot be funded immediately, but will solve the problem permanently in the future when funds are available). A long-term solution can be more cost-effective in the long run that a short-term one.

Estimating Cost

The initial construction cost of protection has two components: fixed and variable. Fixed costs include such items as security hardware and space requirements. These costs do not depend on the level of an attack (i.e., it costs the same to keep a truck away from a building regardless of whether the truck contains 500 or 5,000 pounds of TNT).

Blast protection, on the other hand, is a variable cost. It depends on the threat level, which is a function of the explosive charge weight and the stand-off distance. Building designers have no control over the amount of explosives used, but are able to change the level of protection by defining an appropriate stand-off distance, adopting hardening measures for their buildings, and providing sacrificial spaces that can be affected by terrorist attacks, but, at the same time, can protect people and critical building functions and infrastructure.

The optimal stand-off distance is determined by defining the total cost of protection as the sum of the cost of protection (construction cost) and the cost of stand-off (land cost). These two costs are considered as a function of the stand-off for a given explosive charge weight. The cost of protection is assumed to be proportional to the peak reflected pressure at the building envelope while the cost of land is proportional to the square of the stand-off distance. The optimal level of protection is the one that minimizes the sum of these costs.

If additional land is not available to move the secured perimeter farther from the building, the required floor area of the building can be distributed among additional floors. As the number of floors is increased, the footprint decreases, providing an increased stand-off distance. By balancing the increasing cost of the structure (due to the added floors) and the corresponding decrease in protection cost (due to added stand-off), it is possible to find the optimal number of floors to minimize the cost of protection.

These methods for establishing the best stand-off distance are generally used for the maximum credible explosive charge. If the cost of protection for this charge weight is not within the budgetary constraints, the design charge weight must be modified. A study can be conducted to determine the largest explosive yield and corresponding level of protection that can be incorporated into the building, given the available budget.

Although it is difficult to assign costs to different upgrade measures because they vary, based on the site-specific design, some generalizations can be made. Below is a list of enhancements arranged in order from least expensive to most expensive:

☐ Hardening of unsecured areas

☐ Measures to prevent progressive collapse

☐ Exterior window and wall enhancements

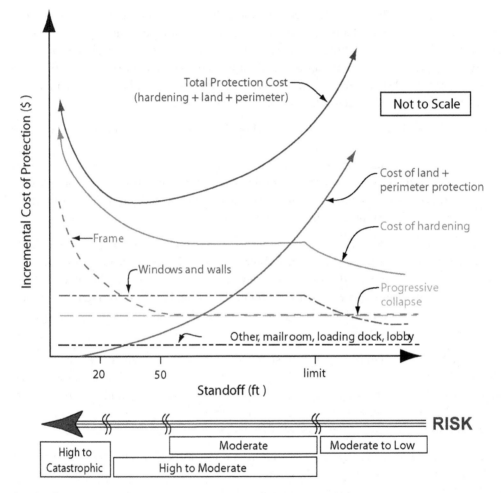

Life-Cycle Costs

Life-cycle costs need to be considered as well. For example, if it is decided that two guarded entrances will be provided, one for visitors and one for employees, they may cost more during the life of the building than a single well designed entrance serving everyone. Also, maintenance costs may need to be considered. For instance, the initial costs for a CBR detection system may be modest, but the maintenance costs are high. Finally, if the rentable square footage is reduced as a result of incorporating robustness into the building, this may have a large impact on the life-cycle costs.

Setting Priorities

> If the costs associated with mitigating manmade hazards are too high there are three approaches available that can be used to combination: (1) reduce the design threat, (2) reduce the level of protection, or (3) accept the risk. In some cases, the owner may decide to prioritize enhancements, based on their effectiveness in saving lives and reducing injuries. For instance, measures against progressive collapse are perhaps the most effective actions that can be implemented to save lives and should be considered above any other upgrades.

Remember

Laminated glass is perhaps the single most effective measure to reduce extensive non-fatal injuries. If the cost is still considered too great, and the risk is high because of the location or the high-profile nature of the building, then the best option may be to consider building an unobtrusive facility in a lower-risk area instead. In some cases (e.g., financial institutions with trading floors), business interruption costs are so high they outweigh all other concerns. In such a case, the most cost-effective solution may be to provide a redundant facility.

Early consideration of manmade hazards will significantly reduce the overall cost of protection and increase the inherent protection level provided to the building. If protection measures are considered as an afterthought or not considered until the design is nearly complete, the cost is likely to be greater, because more areas will need to be structurally hardened. An awareness of the threat of manmade hazards from the beginning of a project also helps the Team to determine early in the process what the priorities are for the facility. For instance, if extensive teak paneling of interior areas visible from the exterior is desired by the architect for the architectural expression of the building, but the cost exceeds that of protective measures, then a decision needs to be made regarding the priorities of the project. Including protective measures as part of the discussion regarding trade-offs early in the design process often helps to clarify such issues.

Applicability of Benefit/Cost to Terrorist Threats

When prioritizing hazard mitigation alternatives, a benefit/cost analysis is generally conducted for each proposed action. A benefit/cost analysis involves calculating the costs of the mitigation measure and weighing them against the intended benefits, frequently expressed as losses avoided. However, applying benefit/cost analysis to terrorist threats can be challenging due to the following three main factors (for more information on this subject, see FEMA 386-7, Integrating Human-Caused Hazards Into Mitigation Planning):

The probability of an attack or frequency is not known. The frequency factor is much more complex in the case of manmade hazards than for natural hazards. Although it is possible to estimate how often many natural disasters will occur (i.e., a structure located in the 100-year floodplain is considered to have a 1 percent chance of being flooded in any given year), it is very difficult to quantify the likelihood of a terrorist attack or technological disaster. Quantitative methods to estimate these probabilities are being developed, but have not yet been refined to the point where they can be used to determine incident probability on a facility-by-facility basis. The Assessment Team may use a qualitative approach based on threat and vulnerability considerations to estimate the relative likelihood of an attack or accident rather than the precise frequency. Such an approach is necessarily subjective, but can be combined with quantitative estimates of cost-effectiveness (the cost of an action compared to the value of the lives and property it saves in a worst-case scenario) to help illustrate the overall risk reduction achieved by a particular mitigation action.

The deterrence rate may not be known. The deterrence or preventive value of a measure cannot be calculated if the number of incidents it averts is not known. Deterrence in the case of terrorism may also have a secondary impact in that, after a potential target is hardened, a terrorist may turn to a less protected facility, changing the likelihood of an attack for both targets.

The lifespan of the action may be difficult to quantify. The lifespan of a mitigation action presents another problem when carrying out a benefit/cost analysis for terrorism and technological hazards. Future benefits are generally calculated for a natural hazard mitigation action in part by estimating the number of times the action will perform successfully over the course of its useful life. However, some protective actions may be damaged or destroyed in a single manmade attack or accident. For example, blast-resistant window film may have performed to 100 percent effectiveness by preventing injuries from flying glass, but it may still need replacement after one "use." Other actions, such as a building setback, cannot be "destroyed" or "used up" per se. This is in contrast to many natural hazard mitigation actions, where the effectiveness and life span of a structural retrofit or land use policy are easily understood and their value over time is quantifiable.

Documentation

As you develop your strategic plan make sure that it is fully documented and that all other relevant documents are updated accordingly. Also make sure that all documents are kept secure. Review the company's emergency response plan and continuation of operations (COOP) plan and make sure that all are compatible and integrated. Then test the plan using drills and make changes if necessary.

Review Process

Writing the strategic plan consists of:

☐ WHY – why changes need to be made and the justification for them

☐ WHAT – what changes need to be made, and

☐ WHEN – when and how the changes will be made (schedule, timeline and budget).

Throughout this process you must keep your plan under constant review. When you are satisfied that it meets all your security objectives and goals, you can move on to Step Five – Implementation.

Summary

In this chapter we reviewed how you set out your strategic plan in order to get management buy in and develop a blueprint for implementing your integrated physical security upgrades. Now we need to implement these measures and that is what the next chapter – the Fifth Step in our methodology – is all about.

STEP FIVE: IMPLEMENTATION

Integrated Execution

Overview

Your facility integrated physical security plan has been accepted by senior management, the funding for it has been approved and now you must implement your strategic plan. Remember that there are three key components to implementation - physical security measures, operations and policies – and all are inter dependent on each other. There is little point in implementing physical security measures such as installing card readers to control access to your facility if you don't carry out background checks (an operational procedure) on your staff to ensure that undesirables are not hired. You also need to have procedures in place (policies) that tell you what to do if a card reader alarm is triggered. These procedures must include training and drills. If there is no training people don't know what to do in an emergency and if there are no drills, how will you know if the systems in place work?

Remember

Operational and Policy Actions

The Project List

Develop a detailed project list. This should correspond to the schedule given in the strategic plan. Start by setting up your project team. Many members of the team may be the same as those chosen for the assessment process but you may need additional expertise to ensure that the construction and installation work is performed to specification. A designer or architect should certainly be involved during this phase and ideally, they should have been part of the time all along. In order to ensure a totally integrated physical security system, make sure that other disciplines are represented on the project team, especially IT, HVAC, electrical and mechanical.

Non-Disclosure

A lot of strangers are going to start working in the facility – from architects and security consultants to contractors and sub-contractors. Make sure that they sign non-disclosure agreements.

Must Do

Working with vendors

Before you can implement your plan you need to select your vendors and contractors – those that will provide the physical security systems and those who will install them and do the other construction work necessary such as physical hardening, erecting barriers and so on.

You need to set the criteria that will be used to select your vendors and contractors, and the guidelines for managing them and you will have to write, or supervise the writing of the requests for proposals.

These guidelines must include the conditions under which the contractors will be employed, what background checks need to be conducted in view of the sensitive nature of the work involved. These guidelines will also apply to all sub contractors employed.

Project Execution

Now you need a project execution plan that will detail the scope of work to be done, the schedule for when it will be done and the budget – how much it will all cost. You have contracted with your vendors and contractors to get the work done and it is now time to start implementation and manage the project.

As project manager you should still rely on your project team, the members of which will all have special responsibilities laid down in the project execution plan.

Project Management – basics

Project management is a formalized and structured method of managing change while introducing specifically designed products (outputs) so that planned benefits (outcomes) are achieved.

Checklist

Key elements of your project should typically be characterized by:

☐ Definable, measurable project outcomes that relate to the organization's goals

☐ Project outputs (required for the attainment of the project outcomes) produced by a your project team(s)

☐ A start date and an end date

☐ A balance between time, cost and quality

☐ A governance structure

☐ Well defined multidisciplinary project team(s)

☐ Involvement of stakeholders/other organizations

☐ Criteria to measure project performance

The key elements that you will have to take into account as project manager are:

☐ Planning and scoping

☐ Governance

☐ Organizational change management

☐ Stakeholder management

☐ Risk management

☐ Issues management

☐ Resource management

☐ Quality management

☐ Status reporting

☐ Evaluation

☐ Closure

It is essential that the project is managed so that the outputs are achieved:

☐ By a certain time

☐ To a defined quality, and

☐ With a given level of resources.

Using sound project management techniques and processes will increase the likelihood that your project will be completed on time, within acceptable level of quality.

Remember that the scope of the project is greater than the work involved. It includes:

☐ Outcomes (long term benefits)

☐ Customers (those who use the outputs)

☐ Outputs (the security systems/measures and procedures generated by the project)

☐ Work (activities and tasks to produce the outputs) and

☐ Resources (human and financial – to get the work done)

You already have in place your planning and management teams who will oversee the project (governance) with each member's specific roles and responsibilities clearly identified.

The project team is not only responsible for implementing the work in hand but its members have a crucial role in ensuring that the changes are adopted as smoothly as possible.

Organizational change management is all about communicating the extent of the changes to all involved and having a plan in hand to manage that change. This will need to address areas such as:

☐ Organizational culture

☐ Physical working environment

☐ Organizational structure

☐ Job design and responsibilities

☐ Skills and knowledge of employees

☐ Employee motivation

☐ Policies and procedures

☐ Workflow and processes, and

☐ Human resource management

All stakeholders have to be involved at every stage of the project's implementation. You should meet with them regularly to keep them informed about progress and to identify and address any concerns they may have.

Next, you need to consider resource management. This is all about managing the people, finances, and the physical and information systems required to execute the project. These may include:

☐ Managing what the people in your team need to do

☐ How and when they do their tasks

☐ Providing suitable accommodation/support for the project team

☐ Producing the outputs

☐ Managing information on a website

☐ Working to an agreed budget, and

☐ Setting up agreements with consultants and contractors and making sure that they deliver.

Note: No matter the size or complexity of the project, it is essential to manage your resources.

You need quality management. You must know before you start work what the desired end result is and then have in place mechanisms and checks to determine whether you are achieving that or not. It is always cheaper and quicker to get it right the first time and this is what quality management is all about. Some of the quality management issues to remember are:

☐ Use valid methodologies and standards

☐ Manage change

☐ Adhere to review and acceptance procedures

☐ Resolve emerging issues

☐ Monitor progress

☐ Engage project staff with the appropriate skills

☐ Maintain appropriate documentation and record keeping

☐ Deliver an output that meets the agreed requirements

☐ Complete the project within budget and on time

As you monitor the project's progress you should issue status reports about what progress has been made and include details about:

- ☐ **Milestones** - what outputs have been delivered, e.g. first draft of document developed
- ☐ **Budget** - how much money has been spent from the budget; does it deviate from the original estimate?
- ☐ **Issues** - areas of concern that may threaten the successful completion of the project, such as tasks not completed by the assigned time (slippage), or not enough people to do the required work.
- ☐ **Risks** - such as the issues that have escalated and are now a threat to the project
- ☐ **Reviews** – you must review the security plan on a regular basis even during implementation to ensure that it is still meeting all your security objectives and goals.

Finally, you need an evaluation management process in place to evaluate the success of the project and ensure that goals are being met. This will also help you determine:

- ☐ Whether the project is on time, on track and on budget (i.e. under control)
- ☐ The level of adherence to documented plans, methodologies and standards
- ☐ Usability of outputs, and
- ☐ The achievement of outcomes

With all these elements in place you are now ready to execute the project. Apart from managing the project you also have another key function – and that is to ensure that the momentum during delivery is sustained. Issues that you need to be concerned with include:

- ☐ Managing people
- ☐ Productivity and quality
- ☐ Meeting deadlines
- ☐ Prioritizing
- ☐ Managing budgets
- ☐ Maintaining enthusiasm
- ☐ Keeping stakeholders involved
- ☐ Contingencies
- ☐ Unexpected problems, and
- ☐ Doing the work to get the job done

Stages in the Life of a Project

Key Element	Initiate	Manage	Finalize
Planning & Scoping	X	X	X
Governance	X	X	X
Organizational Change management	X	X	X
Stakeholder Management	X	X	X
Risk Management	X	X	X
Issues Management		X	X
Resource Management		X	X
Quality Management		X	X
Status Reporting		X	X
Evaluation		X	X
Closure			X

Physical Security Actions

Throughout the execution phase you will need to document the solutions to mitigate the security vulnerabilities, from a broad range of integrated systems. Project execution can be divided into 3 major categories:

☐ **Design** – this is really part of Gap Closure but it provides the blueprint for implementation

■ Bid the project and secure a contractor

☐ **Construction** - a major element of implementation

■ Operations and maintenance

☐ **Commissioning / turnover** – the end of the implementation process

Construction

The construction phase begins with biding out the design packages, awarding the work to a contractor and executing the work. A few key issues to note specific to a security project are:

☐ Background check on labor

■ Temporary security layers during construction phase

■ System integration between hardening & electronic systems

■ Mockups

■ Commissioning

The commissioning phase begins after the security systems are installed and are ready to be tested for the performance they were designed for. Key issues to note:

☐ Different than commissioning equipment, security systems in addition need to be commissioned as integrated components.

☐ For example, an entry portal that includes a turnstile & card reader accesses CCTV and metal detector. Each component should be tested, at the same time the entire portal needs to be tested for scenarios is was designed to mitigate, allowing access of authorized personnel and denying access to adversaries / those who are unauthorized.

☐ Commission the physical hardening and hardware with the related electronics and tie in to facility security systems, i.e. command center etc.

☐ Review the O&M's for the installed systems

☐ Inspect security systems on a regular basis for performance.

Essentially, successful project close involves:

☐ Hand-over of project outputs to the Project Business Owner

☐ Review of project outputs and outcomes against the Project Strategic Plan

☐ Completion or re-assignment of outstanding task

☐ Finalization of project records

☐ Staffing issues e.g. redeploying team members

☐ Confirmation that the benefits of the project have been achieved

☐ 'Tying up the loose ends'

However….

Just because you have successfully implemented your strategic plan, don't think you can now sit back and relax. You have to revisit your plan on a regular basis to ensure that it is still meeting your goals and providing the necessary level of protection. Have the threats changed, are there new threats, are there new and better technologies?

No No

As Katrina proved, you must plan for and be prepared for any eventuality. You have to keep performing "what if" scenarios, carry out regular training and drills and keep in touch with what is going on in and around your facility. In this way, you will have an integrated physical security plan that continues to protect your facility and everyone working in it.

In summary

The key to a smooth execution phase is to begin with a comprehensive plan, following up with integrated design, client involvement, choosing the appropriate solutions that are cost-effective and that meet the overall security objectives.

Remember

After you have completed the security upgrades your goal is to be back to "business as usual" with a higher level of security without any surprises in regards to budget, schedule and end user satisfaction.

Finally, your security program will be constantly challenged due to the nature of ongoing facility changes in operations and building use, therefore a culture of ongoing security reviews must be implemented on an ongoing basis.

Congratulations, you have successfully completed the five steps.

Assessment Checklist

Assessment Checklist	Yes/No	Threat Assessment	Vulnerability Assessment	Risk Assessment	Mitigation Option
		GAP ANALYSIS			GAP CLOSURE
Security Situation		High/ Medium/Low	High/ Medium/Low	High/ Medium/Low	
Your current security situation.					
Are you in a high crime area?					
Are you a high risk target for a terrorist attack?					
Do you store goods, materials that would attract thieves i.e. jewelry store, drugs in a hospital?					
Has your facility ever been broken into?					
Has your facility even been vandalized?					
Have you suffered workplace violence?					
Have you suffered computer/IT crime?					
Do you have an integrated physical security plan?					
Do you have an emergency management plan?					

Assessment Checklist	Yes/No	Threat Assessment	Vulnerability Assessment	Risk Assessment	Mitigation Option
		GAP ANALYSIS			GAP CLOSURE
Security Situation		High/ Medium/Low	High/ Medium/Low	High/ Medium/Low	
2. Site – Neighbors					
Could your neighbors impact on your facility's security					
Am I at risk from facilities in the area i.e. power plants, Government buildings, chemical plants, gas & oil facilities, high risk targets?					
Do nearby roads, railway lines pose a threat?					
Do my immediate neighbors pose a threat i.e. could they be a target, do they handle toxic materials, is there security adequate?					
Do neighborhood development plans impact you?					
3. Site – Location					
How secure is your location					
Is my facility in a favorable location i.e. good all round views, not in a depression, not subject to frequent fogs etc?					
Is my facility in a high traffic urban area (vehicles and pedestrians)?					
Can vehicles park close to my facility?					

Assessment Checklist	Yes/No	Threat Assessment	Vulnerability Assessment	Risk Assessment	Mitigation Option
		GAP ANALYSIS			GAP CLOSURE
Security Situation		High/Medium/Low	High/Medium/Low	High/Medium/Low	
4. Site – Perimeter					
Is my perimeter secure?					
Is there an external perimeter i.e. fence or barriers?					
Is there any stand off distance?					
Are there too many access points to the facility?					
Does vehicle traffic have access to the facility?					
Is vehicle access controlled?					
Is there pedestrian access to the facility?					
Is pedestrian access controlled?					
Is there potential access to the facility from utility paths i.e. manholes, tunnels?					
Is there below ground car parking?					
Is below ground car parking protected?					
Is there good lighting i.e. around the facility, at doorways etc?					
Is there adequate signage in the area?					
Are fire hydrants accessible?					

Assessment Checklist	Yes/No	Threat Assessment	Vulnerability Assessment	Risk Assessment	Mitigation Option
		GAP ANALYSIS			GAP CLOSURE
Security Situation		High/ Medium/Low	High/ Medium/Low	High/ Medium/Low	
Do you have loading bays?					
Are they controlled?					
Are there nearby trashcans/mailboxes?					
5. Perimeter Security					
Do I have adequate perimeter security?					
Is there perimeter security lighting?					
Is there close circuit TV surveillance?					
Are access points monitored?					
6. Building Usage					
Do I understand my building usage?					
Is access to the building controlled?					
Do staff/public use same access points?					
Are all access points protected?					
Does the building have multiple tenants?					
Are public/private areas separated?					
Does the public have access to restrooms/ stairwells/elevators?					
Are access points protected?					
Are critical assets close to the main entrance?					

Assessment Checklist	Yes/No	Threat Assessment	Vulnerability Assessment	Risk Assessment	Mitigation Option
			GAP ANALYSIS		GAP CLOSURE
Security Situation		High/ Medium/Low	High/ Medium/Low	High/ Medium/Low	
Are critical building systems hardened?					
Is internal traffic flow controlled?					
Are critical assets under surveillance?					
Are mail rooms located away from main entrance?					
Is access to mail room controlled?					
Can the mail room be isolated?					
Do you have safe rooms/ areas?					
Do you have different security levels?					
Are there adequate portals between security levels?					
7. Building Structure					
How structurally safe is my facility?					
Does the facility have any physical hardening i.e. reinforced walls, floors, doors etc?					
Do the windows have strengthened glass?					
Could the walls withstand an external or internal explosion?					
Are non weight bearing walls reinforced?					

Assessment Checklist	Yes/No	Threat Assessment	Vulnerability Assessment	Risk Assessment	Mitigation Option
		GAP ANALYSIS			GAP CLOSURE
Security Situation		High/ Medium/Low	High/ Medium/Low	High/ Medium/Low	
Are critical elements subject to failure?					
Is the structure vulnerable to collapse?					
Are there adequate redundant load paths in the structure?					
Is the loading dock able to withstand/contain an explosion?					
Is the mailroom able to withstand/contain an explosion?					
8. Utility Systems					
Understanding your utilities					
Do you know the source of domestic water i.e. utility, municipal, storage tank?					
Is there a secure alternate drinking water supply?					
Do you know how the water comes into the facility i.e. one point/ multiple points?					
Are the water entry points secure?					
Do you know the source of water for the fire suppression system i.e. utility line, storage tanks, river etc?					
Is the fire suppression system adequate?					

Assessment Checklist	Yes/No	Threat Assessment	Vulnerability Assessment	Risk Assessment	Mitigation Option
			GAP ANALYSIS		GAP CLOSURE
Security Situation		High/ Medium/Low	High/ Medium/Low	High/ Medium/Low	
Are sprinkler and standpipe connections adequate and redundant?					
Are sewer systems accessible?					
Are sewer systems protected?					
Do you know what fuels the building relies on for critical operations?					
Do you know how much fuel is stored on site?					
Is storage secure and protected?					
Do you know how fuel is delivered?					
Are there alternate sources of fuel?					
Do you know your normal source of electricity?					
Is there a redundant electrical source?					
Do you know how many electric service points there are?					
Are these electric service points secure?					
Are there provisions for emergency power?					
Are there transformers or switchgear outside the building?					
Are they vulnerable to public access?					

Assessment Checklist	Yes/No	Threat Assessment	Vulnerability Assessment	Risk Assessment	Mitigation Option
		GAP ANALYSIS			GAP CLOSURE
Security Situation		High/ Medium/Low	High/ Medium/Low	High/ Medium/Low	
Are they protected?					
Is the electrical room protected?					
Are critical electrical systems collocated with other building systems?					
Do you know how telephone and data communications come into the building?					
Are these access points secure?					
Are there redundancies in telephone and data communications?					
Is your fire alarm system reliant on external communications?					
Are fire alarm panels protected?					
Are fire alarm systems standalone or integrated with other systems?					
Are utility lines above ground/underground or buried?					
Are external air intakes accessible to the public?					
Are these air intakes protected?					
Can air intakes be closed/ sealed?					
Do you have air monitors/sensors?					

Assessment Checklist	Yes/No	Threat Assessment	Vulnerability Assessment	Risk Assessment	Mitigation Option
		GAP ANALYSIS			GAP CLOSURE
Security Situation		High/ Medium/Low	High/ Medium/Low	High/ Medium/Low	
Can sections of the AC be isolated?					
Is roof access limited?					
Are mechanical systems in secure areas?					
Are there smoke evacuation systems?					
Do you have fire barriers?					
Are there fire dampers at all fire barriers?					
Can elevators by shut down and isolated?					
Is access to building materials controlled?					
9. People					
What do you know about your most critical asset?					
Do you know who uses your facility i.e. staff, tenants, visitors, deliveries etc?					
Do you know traffic flow patterns to and around the building?					
Do you know traffic flows within the building?					
Do employees carry ID cards?					
Are there access controls for employees entering the building i.e. badges/ cards etc?					

Assessment Checklist	Yes/No	Threat Assessment	Vulnerability Assessment	Risk Assessment	Mitigation Option
		GAP ANALYSIS			GAP CLOSURE
Security Situation		High/Medium/Low	High/Medium/Low	High/Medium/Low	
Are there different security layers within the building?					
Is access to these different layers controlled?					
Are visitors screened and searched?					
Do you have security staff?					
Do you have front desk security?					
Do you do background checks on all employees?					
Do employees understand the need for security?					
Do you practice security/fire/evacuation drills?					
10. Communications and IT					
How secure are my communications and IT?					
Is the main telephone distribution room secure?					
Does the room have an uninterruptible power supply?					
Is communications wiring secure?					
Are there redundant communication systems?					
Is the IT main distribution location secure?					

Assessment Checklist	Yes/No	Threat Assessment	Vulnerability Assessment	Risk Assessment	Mitigation Option
		GAP ANALYSIS			GAP CLOSURE
Security Situation		High/ Medium/Low	High/ Medium/Low	High/ Medium/Low	
Do IT systems meet requirements for integrity, confidentiality and availability?					
Is there a disaster recovery mirroring site?					
Is back up for tapes/file storage safe?					
Is there a mass notification system to reach all building occupants i.e. public address, pagers?					
11. Equipment Operation & Maintenance					
What do I need to know about my building systems?					
Are there plans of all major systems?					
Are all plans current?					
Are there updated operations & maintenance manuals?					
Have critical air systems been rebalanced?					
Are mechanical/electrical/ plumbing (MEP) systems tested and balanced on a regular basis?					
Are there maintenance and service agreements for MEP?					
Are back up power systems tested regularly?					

Assessment Checklist	Yes/No	Threat Assessment	Vulnerability Assessment	Risk Assessment	Mitigation Option
		GAP ANALYSIS			GAP CLOSURE
Security Situation		High/ Medium/Low	High/ Medium/Low	High/ Medium/Low	
Do all stairway and emergency exit lights work?					
12. External Security Systems					
Do I have the right external protection?					
Are close circuit TVs in use?					
Are they monitored and recorded 24/7?					
Do they have an uninterrupted power supply?					
Do the cameras respond automatically to perimeter alarm events?					
Do the cameras have built in video motion capabilities?					
Are panic/duress alarm buttons used?					
Are their intercom call boxes in parking areas and along the building perimeter?					
Is there adequate monitoring of the CCTV?					
Are infrared camera illuminators used?					
Are there exterior intrusion detection system sensors (IDS) i.e. electromagnetic, fiber optic, active infrared, microwave etc?					

Assessment Checklist	Yes/No	Threat Assessment	Vulnerability Assessment	Risk Assessment	Mitigation Option
		GAP ANALYSIS			GAP CLOSURE
Security Situation		High/ Medium/Low	High/ Medium/Low	High/ Medium/Low	
Is GPS used to monitor vehicles?					
13. Internal Security Systems					
Do I have the right internal protection?					
Are CCTVs used?					
Are they monitored 24/7?					
Do they monitor the whole building?					
Are they programmed to respond automatically to interior building alarm events?					
Is the transmission media i.e. fiber, telephone wire, wireless etc. secure?					
Is there a security access control system?					
Are physical security systems integrated with IT networks?					
What is the alternate backup power supply for the access control systems?					
Are panic/duress alarm buttons used?					
Are there intercom call boxes in the building?					
Are metal detectors/X-ray equipment used?					
Are interior IDS sensors used?					

Assessment Checklist	Yes/No	Threat Assessment	Vulnerability Assessment	Risk Assessment	Mitigation Option
		GAP ANALYSIS			GAP CLOSURE
Security Situation		High/ Medium/Low	High/ Medium/Low	High/ Medium/Low	
Do you know what locks are used in the building i.e. manual, electromagnetic, keypad etc?					
Are potentially hazardous materials kept on site?					
Are there security procedures for handling mail?					
Is there a designated security room?					
Is there a backup security room?					
Is there offsite 24/7 monitoring of IDSs?					
Is the security room in a secure area?					
Are there vaults or safes in the building?					
Are they protected?					
14. Security System Documents					
Are my critical documents current and available?					
Are security system as-built drawings available?					
Are security system manuals available?					
Have security system design and drawing standards been developed?					
Are security equipment selection criteria defined?					

Assessment Checklist	Yes/No	Threat Assessment	Vulnerability Assessment	Risk Assessment	Mitigation Option
		GAP ANALYSIS			GAP CLOSURE
Security Situation		High/ Medium/Low	High/ Medium/Low	High/ Medium/Low	
Have contingency plans been developed?					
Have security system construction plans been prepared and standardized?					
Have qualifications been determined for security consultants, system designers, engineers, installation vendors & contractors?					
15. Security Master Plan					
Master plan critical issues					
Is there a written system security plan for the building?					
Has it been recently reviewed and revised?					
Has the plan been communicated to key management?					
Has the plan been benchmarked against related organizations and operational entities?					
Has the security plan be tested and evaluated from a benefit/cost and operational efficiency/ effective perspectives?					
Does the plan set out short/medium/long term goals and objectives?					

Assessment Checklist	Yes/No	Threat Assessment	Vulnerability Assessment	Risk Assessment	Mitigation Option
		GAP ANALYSIS			GAP CLOSURE
Security Situation		High/ Medium/Low	High/ Medium/Low	High/ Medium/Low	
Have security operating and capital budgets been addressed?					
Have all regulatory and industry guidelines been followed?					
Does the security plan address the protection of people, property, critical assets & information?					
Does the plan address access control, response, surveillance, building hardening and protection against CBR and cyber-network attacks?					
Do you know when the last security assessment was carried out?					
Does the plan address all issues flagged by the asset, threat, vulnerability & risk assessments?					
16. Compliance					
Are all your upgrades and measures code compliant?					

CRITICAL ASSET WORKSHEET #1 FORM

Asset Type	Redundant sys/ Backup?	Criticality/ Priority (1-10)	Above threshold Y/N
People			
Operations			
Information			
Interdependencies			

DESIGN BASIS THREAT WORKSHEET #2 FORM

Adversary List/type	Motive	Profile/ Characteristics	Probability of Attack		
			Low	Medium	High

FACILITY VULNERABILITY ASSESSMENT WORKSHEET #3 FORM

Scenario no:_____   Adversary/ Threat_____

Legend

☐ Critical Asset	☐ Site Access	☐ _____	☐ _____
☐ Buildings	☐ Bld Access	☐ _____	☐ _____
☐ On Site parking	☐ Roads	☐ _____	☐ _____
☐ Fencing	☐ Security Cameras	☐ _____	☐ _____
☐ Lighting	☐ Roads	☐ _____	☐ _____

SCENARIO ASSESSMENT WORKSHEET #4 FORM

Scenario no:_____   Adversary/ Threat_____

Adversary Attack	Allowing Systems - Vulnerabilities	Type of System

SCENARIO V MITIGATION WORKSHEET #5 FORM

Scenario no:_____   Adversary/ Threat_____

Vulnerability	Gap Closure/ Mitigation Concept	Mitigation Catagory			
		Detect	Delay	Assess	Respond

MASTER MITIGATION WORKSHEET #6 FORM

Gap Closure/ Mitigation Concept	New or Tie-in to existing systems	ROM $ Estimate			
		1st Cost	Recurring	Ops. Cost	Total Cost

CPSIA information can be obtained
at www.ICGtesting.com
Printed in the USA
LVOW03s0003090616

491801LV00005B/15/P